EMBRACING
EXILE

*Living Faithfully as God's
Unique People in the World*

T. SCOTT DANIELS

BEACON HILL PRESS
OF KANSAS CITY

Copyright © 2017 by T. Scott Daniels

Beacon Hill Press of Kansas City
PO Box 419527
Kansas City, MO 64141
www.BeaconHillBooks.com

ISBN 978-0-8341-3643-4

Printed in the
United States of America

Cover Design: Arthur Cherry
Interior Design: Sharon Page

Scriptures marked CEB are from the *Common English Bible.* Copyright © 2011 by the Common English Bible. All rights reserved. Used by permission. (www.CommonEnglishBible .com <http://www.CommonEnglishBible.com>).

Scriptures marked NIV are from the *Holy Bible, New International Version*® (NIV®). Copyright © 1973, 1978, 1984, 2011 by Biblica, Inc.® Used by permission. All rights reserved worldwide.

Scriptures marked NRSV are from the *New Revised Standard Version Bible,* copyright © 1989 National Council of the Churches of Christ in the United States of America. Used by permission. All rights reserved.

Library of Congress Cataloging-in-Publication Data
Names: Daniels, T. Scott, 1966- author.
Title: Embracing exile : living faithfully as God's unique people in the world / T. Scott Daniels.
Description: Kansas City, MO : Beacon Hill Press of Kansas City, 2017. |
   Includes bibliographical references.
Identifiers: LCCN 2016051191 | ISBN 9780834136434 (pbk.)
Subjects: LCSH: Identification (Religion) | Christianity and culture. | Exiles—Religious life. |
Religious refugees.
Classification: LCC BV4509.5 .D249 2017 | DDC 261—dc23 LC record available at
https://lccn.loc.gov/2016051191

The Internet addresses, email addresses, and phone numbers in this book are accurate at the time of publication. They are provided as a resource. Beacon Hill Press of Kansas City does not endorse them or vouch for their content or permanence.

10 9 8 7 6 5 4 3 2 1

For Caleb:

Whose different spirit is a blessing to his mother and me.

I'll bring my servant Caleb into the land that he explored,
*and his descendants will possess it because **he has a different spirit,***
and he has remained true to me.

—Num. 14:24, CEB, emphasis added

CONTENTS

INTRODUCTION

Exile is the way to new life in new land. One can scarcely imagine a more radical, less likely understanding of history. In covenantal categories, **embrace of curse is the root to blessing.** In New Testament categories, **embrace of death is the way to life.** . . . Jeremiah announces the central scandal of the Bible, that radical loss and discontinuity do happen and are the source of real newness. So he holds what surely must have been a minority view, that the exiles *are the real* heirs. *And conversely those who cling to the land are the ultimate exiles.*

—Walter Brueggemann, *The Land*, emphasis added

● ● ●

I first started thinking and speaking about exile a little over a decade ago when I accepted the call to pastor the wonderful people at Pasadena First Church of the Nazarene in Southern California (affectionately known in the community as PazNaz). At that time the century-old congregation, with such a rich history and beautiful facilities, had been through significant shifts and challenges, and some people were not sure that it had much of a future.

As I prepared to try and lead the church forward, I knew I was in over my head. In my desperation, I felt led to preach in those early days in Pasadena from the Old Testament narratives of exile.

So many of the fears the people of God faced in Babylon—fears that the glory days were over, fears that their children were being lost to the surrounding culture, fears that all the symbols and practices of God's work in the past would disappear—seemed to resonate with the realities we were facing as a church.

What I believe we discovered in those days listening to the voices of our ancestors of faith in exile was not just a way to narrate the present but a way to allow the Spirit of God to form new patterns of imagination for the future. I suppose the gift we most needed that those texts from Judah and Israel's past offered was hope.

Because of the joy and new creation that we as a church rediscovered in the great narratives of exile and hope, I started preaching those same texts elsewhere as I had opportunity. The more I preached about exile, the more it became clear to me that the themes emerging from the stories of Egypt, Babylon, and first-century Rome were speaking deeply to people and churches in a wide variety of cultural contexts.

I also found in the books I was picking up—ranging from the academic to the pastoral—that the themes of exile were helping many people to narrate and navigate the church as a unique people in the midst of a rapidly changing and increasingly secular culture.

So this book and the materials that accompany it are an attempt to merge together a decade or so of reflection on the biblical moments of exile, how those themes might be speaking anew to the cultural context of today, and how those narratives might offer to the contemporary church hopeful ways of living as kingdom people in a world that feels more and more strange.

People who live in exile feel displaced. They feel like resident aliens. They feel like a people who have to live counterculturally.

The thesis, if you will, of this study is that this sense of out-of-placeness is actually the way disciples of Jesus ought to feel. Faithful followers of Christ who have taken up their cross to follow him will always embody a kind of life the world cannot understand in its own terms. The kingdom of God always breaks into creation in subversive and overlooked ways.

Let me state up front that exile is not a perfect metaphor. Like all metaphors, it breaks down in certain—and sometimes significant—places. So let me go ahead and name some of those limitations.

Exile is not a perfect metaphor because exile is usually about being picked up and physically relocated into places of unfamiliarity and alienation. Most of us haven't been taken anywhere. In whatever way exile as a metaphor may speak to the twenty-first-century church, it will be because there is a feeling that things have changed in places of familiarity, not because we were taken away to foreign lands. Most of us are more akin to frogs miraculously realizing the water in the kettle around them is beginning to boil than like people who have been taken from their homes and forcibly moved as aliens to a strange land.

It isn't a perfect metaphor because most Christians—especially in Europe and North America—have not been completely displaced from roles of influence and authority in their nations and cultures. Although some may feel a loss of power, Christians cannot fully separate themselves from the political responsibilities and decisions of the nations and cultures of which they are a part.

I especially feel a twinge of awkwardness describing my own social and religious setting in exilic terms when compared to the very real forms of exile, marginalization, and ostracism that many of the world's refugees, minorities, and persecuted people have experienced in the past or are currently living through. If the language of exile is just one more way for privileged people to whine about their aversion to change, then the metaphor of exile not only breaks down but also becomes unhelpful. There is indeed much to learn about faithfulness from those who have been forced to sustain fidelity to Christ in the midst of very real threats to their existence.

Most of all, the metaphor of exile breaks down if it is heard as a cry for Christians to continue fighting to retain or recapture the church's former positions of power. Using the language of exile is not a clarion call to return to the Constantinian synthesis of the church and the world's principalities and powers. To quote from Stanley Hauerwas and William Willimon's seminal work on exile—*Resident Aliens*,

> The demise of the Constantinian world view, the gradual decline of the notion that the church needs some sort of "Christian" culture to prop it up and mold its young, is not a death to lament. It is an opportunity to celebrate. The decline of the old, Constantinian synthesis between the church and the world means that we American Christians are at last free to be faithful in a way that makes being a Christian today an exciting adventure.[1]

Despite these limitations, I am convinced that recapturing and even embracing the language and images of the biblical theme of exile may help the church not only narrate some of the cultural changes taking place but more importantly help the church rediscover the unique and often subversive kingdom life to which the people of God have always been called.

My hope is that recapturing exile as a metaphor will help the church hear anew the prophetic tradition of Scripture. The prophets help God's people put on new and often radical lenses of interpretation that unmask the way we have been shaped by the principalities and powers. The prophets invite God's people to confess their past sins and failures. The prophets invite God's people to hope in the Creator's creative ability to re-create out of the broken pieces of history. But most of all the prophets invite God's people to lament and release what has happened in the past in order to receive the new thing that the Lord is doing in their midst.

As Old Testament scholar Walter Brueggemann ironically states in the quote that opens this introduction, "Exile is the way to new life in new land."[2] One of the radical claims of the prophets is that the exile God's people face comes not from an accident in history but directly from the hand of God. Nebuchadnezzar—in all of his idolatry—was an unwitting instrument whom God was using to impel his people into new creation. As Brueggemann states, the possibilities for new life occur only out of the "embrace of curse" or, in New Testament terms, in the "embrace of death."[3]

So I want to invite the church to *embrace exile.* Whatever dislocation, uncertainty, and disempowerment the church may be experiencing in the present may indeed be an act of God helping his people to experience anew the possibilities of covenantal faithfulness. Like Joseph affirms to his brothers after his identity in Egypt was made known to them, what may seem as if it is intended for evil may in fact be God's good act of salvation in disguise (see Gen. 50:20).

This study is meant to invite congregations into conversation with the Spirit of God and with one another. For this reason questions for discussion are included at the end of each chapter, and online resources have been put together to connect with this study so that pastors, congregations, small groups, and especially people from different generations, genders, and ethnicities can wrestle together with how the biblical themes of exile may narrate the particular slice of the world around them.

Most importantly, this study is intended to help the people of God discover what faithfulness looks like and how holiness is possible, even when the surrounding culture fails to support or may even mistreat those committed to Christ as Lord. As this study will observe more than once, even though exile is *not* a social location people desire to live in, the people of God are usually at their best when they are forced to live as "a chosen race, a royal priesthood, a holy nation, God's own people" (1 Pet. 2:9, NRSV).

The first chapter of this study explores exile as a biblical theme and begins imagining how this theme might narrate this historical moment for the church.

The second chapter is about ecclesiology. The word *ecclesiology* simply means the "study of the church." One of the benefits of exile is that it forces the people of God to recover their identity as a unique people. In times past, certain nations could think of themselves as "Christian nations"; thus they could sometimes identify their citizens as Christian by default. In exile, however, nations such as Egypt, Babylon, or Rome are no longer "home" for God's people. The people may be citizens in that country, but their true heart and home belongs with those who worship the world's one true Lord, whose kingdom transcends all national borders and boundaries. That's an ecclesiology—a counterculture—that can endure through exile.

There are two key things that a people must have in order to survive and thrive in exile. Those two things are a forming story and sustaining practices. The third chapter is devoted to describing, in broad detail, how the world lost a shared story and how the church can live into God's counterstory of redemption, salvation, and sanctification. The fourth chapter focuses on the key practices that keep the people of God from being "conformed to this world" in order to be "transformed by the renewing of [their] minds" (Rom. 12:2, NRSV).

Chapter 5 is about how God's people in exile are called to work for the good of the place where they are, even if it is not their home. God does not expect his people to try to escape their location or live in seclusion from it. Rather, the biblical call is for God's people to "work for the good of Babylon" (see Jer. 29:7).[4] So we must discover how to work in ways that glorify God and bless others.

One of the greatest fears for a people in exile is that they will lose their children to the culture. I am convinced one of the key reasons God's people started preserving Scripture as sacred was so they could use it to form the next generation into resident aliens as well. Raising resident aliens is a huge challenge. Thus the sixth chapter focuses on spiritual formation—especially of the church's young people—in exile.

Finally, although the church has always had a mission, in a sense the church has also always been a mission. The goal of the church in exile is not simply to survive in order to get to the other side someday but to live within exile as a countermissional people, extending salt and light to a broken world. Therefore, the last chapter springs from the prophet Isaiah's wonderful word of hope to exiles.

[The Lord] says,
"It is too light a thing that you should be my servant
    to raise up the tribes of Jacob
    and to restore the survivors of Israel;

I will give you as a light to the nations,

that my salvation may reach to the end of the earth."

(Isa. 49:6, NRSV)

My hope is that interpreting our current historical moment through the lens of exile will not only spark our imaginations toward unique faithfulness in a perilous time but also awaken within the church new hopes for God's glory to be revealed in and through his "chosen race," his "royal priesthood," his "holy nation" (1 Pet. 2:9, NRSV). So may we embrace exile, and may God's newness embrace us.

1

STRANGERS IN A STRANGE TIME

Tevye: As Abraham said, "I am a stranger in a strange land. . . ."
Mendel: Moses said that.
*Tevye: Ah. Well, as King David said, "I am slow of speech, and
slow of tongue."*
Mendel: That was also Moses.
Tevye: For a man who was slow of tongue, he talked a lot.
—Fiddler on the Roof

● ● ●

They shall go into exile, into captivity.
—Ezekiel 12:11, NRSV

● ● ●

I once had a parishioner say to me, "Pastor, I know the world is much different than the one I was raised in. And I know the church has to change to face those new realities. But do you think we could wait to change until after I die?" I think that dear saint was joking. But the ever-increasing sensation of disorientation in the world isn't very funny.

Many Christians are waking up to the reality that they are suddenly strangers in a strange time. The reality of how odd a time we are living in hit me just a few years ago when I was trying to start a lecture in my theology course but the students weren't having any of it. At the time, I was serving as the dean of the school of theology at a large Christian university in Southern California. It was early in the academic year, but the school was already in chaos.

Just a few days into the school year one of the theology faculty at the university, after years of battling depression, abuse, instability, and dysphoria, announced that she was transgender and that over her spring sabbatical and summer she had come to embrace her identity as a transgender person. At that time she was in the early stages of transitioning medically and legally to a male identity.

The next few weeks and months were filled with turmoil and tension as those of us in leadership at the university tried to balance care for this individual with the historic faith commitments of the university. There were other challenges as well. There were challenges navigating the attacks from the local and national media, who never seemed to tell the story accurately. There was the challenge of dealing with the deeply felt emotions and diverse opinions of faculty not only in the school of theology but also in the university as a whole. There was the challenge of responding to a divided constituency of Christian friends and alumni of the university.

And on a university campus there was also the great challenge of dealing with the questions and concerns of students.

The unease of these circumstances leads me back to the class session I will never forget. That day, early in the process, my students simply wouldn't let me lecture. They had too many questions. And although they knew there were many things that I could not say because of my position at the school, they needed someone in authority to talk with them. It turned out to be a difficult, respectful, and important hour and a half.

What struck me most in that impromptu class discussion was how "at home" the students were living in this difficult situation and having this hard conversation. Most could not understand why so many of the adults involved were not as comfortable.

I tried to tell them that despite all of my years of theological and ministerial study, from undergraduate school to seminary, nothing prepared me for the decisions I was making and the cultural tensions I was navigating. I tried to help them understand that if the students could just step back in time thirty, forty, or fifty years and walk across that same campus with the alumni who were now stakeholders and trustees, they would experience a very different world. I tried to help them appreciate that when many of the constituents of this particular holiness university were students, the primary issues on campus were dorm curfews, the length of women's skirts, and the propriety of wearing jeans to class. The majority of the students were almost incapable of imagining how radically the university culture had changed in just a few decades. And they were also hard-pressed to empathize with the plight of administration, faculty, and alumni who were having such a difficult time understanding the religious, political, social, and cultural diversity and complexity at work on a campus where not too long ago life had seemed fairly simple and Mayberryesque.

As I tried to explain the massive changes that had taken place just in that corner of Southern California, I realized the students were looking at me as if I were from Mars. But that's okay, because they also seemed to me like aliens from a world that I barely understood.

That feeling, as Christians, that we are living in a world that we struggle to understand, that no longer seems to speak the language of historic Christian faith, and over which we feel very little control is rapidly becoming the norm and not the exception. Like Moses, many of us feel like strangers in a strange land.

The Bible has a way of narrating the oddness that the people of God often feel in the world. The Scriptures call it exile.

Exile

I once heard a student ask Old Testament scholar Walter Brueggemann how he could write about so many different places in the Bible. His answer went something like this: "Years ago I discovered that there was only one story in the Bible; that story just gets repeated over and over again. The primary story in Scripture is that God has called a people to be his reflection—his image—in the world. The problem is that those people always live in an empire that keeps trying to shape them in ways contrary to the ways of God. So every place in the Bible is trying to answer this question: How can we live as God's unique people in the midst of this place that lives so contrary to his purposes?"

Brueggemann was implying to the student that almost the entire Bible speaks to the people of God while they are in exile. Think about all of the places of exile in the Scriptures:

- God asked Abraham and Sarah to leave all of their places of security and protection and to follow him into unfamiliar places.
- In Egypt Pharaoh enslaved the people and mistreated them.
- In the Promised Land God's people lived surrounded by foreign and violent nations.
- Assyria conquered the northern nation of Israel or Ephraim.
- Babylon conquered Judah and took the people into captivity.
- The first-century Jewish people lived under the authority of Rome.

It would seem as though God's people have almost always had to narrate their life through the lens of exile.

The Jewish people think of history as moving in a linear direction. They believe history had a beginning ("In the beginning God created . . ." [Gen. 1:1, NIV]), and it will someday have an end ("He who testifies to these things says, 'Yes, I am coming soon.' Amen" [Rev. 22:20, NIV]). However, I would like to propose that as history moves in a linear direction from its beginning to its end, it also seems to move in a kind of spiral or looping fashion. History, for the people of God, moves forward in what I will call a *hermeneutical circle*—which is a fancy way of saying life has a funny habit of repeating itself, and as it repeats itself, we can interpret various movements along the way. The following chart of Israel's early history may help this make sense.

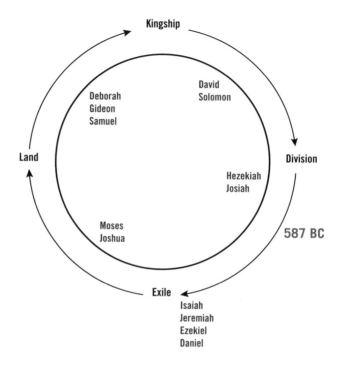

If you think of the chart above as a clock, the hermeneutical cycle for Israel begins at the bottom—at the six o'clock position—with the word *Exile*. Although the story of God's people began with the call of Abraham, in a sense its first moment as a nation was when the Lord delivered the descendants of Abraham, Isaac, and Jacob from Egypt.

The chart then moves clockwise to the nine o'clock position—with the word *Land*. As you will notice on the chart, as the people moved from slavery in exile to freedom in the land, they needed and were given by God unique leaders. In this case they were given

Moses and Joshua, who—like mythic superheroes—led the people into places they had never gone before.

The chart then moves to the twelve o'clock position and the time called *Kingship*. You will notice that leaders (judges) such as Deborah, Gideon, and Samuel are noted because they helped the people move through the rugged days of early establishment and transitioned them into the stability of kingship. In the period of kingship David and his son Solomon were certainly the ones who set the imagination for what great kings ought to be like. Kingship is at the top of the cycle chart because this time period (around 1000 BC) is considered to be the pinnacle of power, wealth, influence, and security for the nation of Israel. If exile was the worst of times, kingship was the best of times.

Or was it?

There is a biblical shadow that hangs over this kingship period. When the people came to Samuel to demand a king, neither he nor God was thrilled about this idea (see 1 Sam. 8). God warned the people that the taxes were going to be high (April 15 rolls around every year), that kings like to fight wars using the sons of the people, and that the king will make the daughters of the people part of his household. He also warned them that having a human king would erode the unique spiritual dynamic that came with depending on God for their security and direction. But the people declared that they wanted to "be like all the other nations" (v. 20, NIV), and they demanded a king.

Even though David had a heart after God, and Solomon was gifted with God's wisdom, they both turned out to be less than stellar leaders. David wrote nice psalms, but he was also an adulterer, a murderer, and a pretty lousy father. Solomon could solve disputes like a master, but he also did all five things the Torah (in Deut. 17) commanded that a king not do: he acquired too many horses and chariots, he returned to Egypt to buy them, he became obsessed with accumulating gold, he took numerous foreign wives, and he turned the heart of the people away from fidelity to God.

It only took three kings—Saul, David, and Solomon—for the burden of kingship to become too much and the nation to divide in two. That moves us to the three o'clock position on the chart. During the time of the division between Ephraim (or Israel) and Judah the Bible narrates the stories of lots of less-than-stellar kings. There were, however, a few exceptions. I list my two favorite kings—Hezekiah and Josiah—on the chart as examples of great leaders who led momentary revivals among the people of God. But when the reader encounters their stories, he or she can clearly see that the Scripture writers were convinced there was no way to reverse the momentum in the hermeneutical circle. Despite momentary rebirths, the trajectory of history is headed for a return trip into exile.

The date 587 BC has been placed on the chart because in many ways it is the date of no return. The northern nation of Israel or Ephraim was destroyed by the Assyrians in 722 BC, and although Judah and its capital city of Jerusalem were able to hold the Assyrians at bay, once Nebuchadnezzar conquered the southern nation in 587 BC, there was no turning back. After 587 BC, no king—no matter how moral—would make a difference. Exile was once again the reality for the people of God.

In and around exile critical new voices emerged for Israel's life and future. Trailblazers, judges, and kings could not offer much help in captivity. In exile the people needed the prophets to speak. Certainly the twelve books called the Minor Prophets have their place in narrating exile for the people. But I have listed the four major prophets—Isaiah, Jeremiah, Ezekiel, and Daniel—as the key exilic leaders. In exile the prophets helped the people lament. In exile the prophets called the people to maintain their identity. In exile the prophets inspired the people to dream new dreams. And in exile the prophets restored hope in God's faithfulness. If the people had failed to listen to the prophets, very likely their history would have ended in exile. But if they could hear the voice of the Lord speaking through his odd messengers, not only could they endure their alienation, but there in a strange land they might also discover anew God's hopes for them when they would return to the land. The words of the prophets might even help the people imagine being part of a new kingdom led by a very different kind of king.

It is certainly fascinating to think about how the experience of exile shaped and formed the imagination of God's people. But it should also raise the question, if we were to narrate our own historical situation in the light of the hermeneutical circle above, where would we place ourselves?

Over these last few years, as I have posed that question to many brothers and sisters in Christ, something about the theme of exile seems to resonate with our current experience. Although—as I detailed in the introduction—the metaphor of exile has significant limitations, there is something about living with oddness, with a feeling of not having control culturally, and with a sense that the Christian story shapes the imagination of fewer and fewer people that sounds the echoes of exile.

One additional reservation I have about equating this historical moment with Israel's exile is that I don't know for certain if culturally speaking we've had our 587 BC turning-point moment. In *Resident Aliens*, Hauerwas and Willimon muse that they think the world officially changed on a Sunday evening in 1963 when in Greenville, South Carolina, "in defiance of the state's time-honored blue laws, the Fox Theater opened on Sunday."[1] That night Will and some of his friends entered the front door of the church so they could be seen and then slipped out the back so they could worship at the theater with John Wayne. As Willimon writes, "On that night, Greenville, South Carolina—the last pocket of resistance to secularity in the Western world—served notice that it would no longer be a prop for the church. . . . The Fox Theater went head to head with the church over who would provide the world view for the young. That night in 1963, the Fox Theater won the opening skirmish."[2]

I don't know if the end of blue laws in the southern United States fully qualifies as the church's 587 BC moment. More recently, some have been pointing to the 2015 Supreme Court decision on same-sex marriage as the moment the culture informed the church it was no longer in charge. That could be. My guess is that our grandchildren will let us know if and when we had our 587 BC moment. What I do know is that there is an increasing sense for many in the Christian church that we are strangers in a strange time.

Concerns in Exile

If the exile metaphor is beginning to resonate with you, there are some questions or concerns that are unique to exile that we probably ought to wrestle with. There are certainly lots of challenges for the people of God in exile, but let me briefly mention what I think are some key concerns.

First, there is almost always a sense among an exiled people that the "glory" of God's unique presence is gone and may never come back. People in exile quite naturally lament the loss of control, power, and peace associated with the "good old days." Let me state again that exile is not a metaphor to be adopted by those who are unhappy or simply want to whine about how much things change or who often forget how the "good old days" weren't very good for a lot of people. Nevertheless, there is a creeping sense among many in the American church in particular that the best days of the church in this culture are behind it and that the trajectory is not an optimistic one.

Exile also brings a loss of practices, habits, and places of familiarity. Think about the Judeans in exile trying to continue their worship of God, only now there was no Holy City (Jerusalem), no temple in which to worship, and none of the rituals of the priestly tradition to rely on.

Third, living in exile is morally complex. Exiled people have to figure out how to live with neighbors whose worldview and moral code is very different from their own. When a community thinks the same way and shares the same convictions, moral judgments are fairly easy to make. But when multiple sets of convictions come together, it makes decisions and shared perspectives more challenging. In exile, moral decision-making can quickly become a struggle for power rather than the shared pursuit of truth.

In exile, slipping into despair also is easy. Hope is essential for people who feel displaced. But hope is not always easy to find.

Finally, in exile, one of the primary fears is the loss of children. One of the challenges during the Babylonian exile in particular (and the reason I believe the Revelator chose Babylon as the metaphor to narrate first-century Rome) is that the surrounding culture is so alluring. Exile in Egypt was oppressive. Unlike Pharaoh, however, Nebuchadnezzar wanted the best and the brightest of Judah to integrate and become leaders in his new empire. One of the great fears of the Judeans in exile was that God would deliver them from Babylon but that their children would choose to stay in this place that had now shaped their identity.

Think about how these same fears shape so many of us in our current context. How many people in your congregation remember the glory of the "good old days" and worry that the spiritual dynamic of those transformative moments are gone forever? How often have you heard people lament the loss of familiar practices that they identify with God's presence and movement in the past? Can you think of a time in recent history when the pastoral decisions were as complex and challenging as they are right now? Do you sense the despair and fears of people sitting in the pews each week? How many books come out each year about the missing generations in the church and how the church fears that children raised as Christians are being drawn deeper into the culture rather than deeper into the faith?

I think these are all signs of the growing sense of exile among the people of God today.

So what do we do?

The rest of this study will contain six suggestions for how the people of God not only sustained their life through exile but also actually thrived and were blessed during that difficult time. The first suggestion will be that we rediscover the life of the church as a community. In the next chapter I will suggest that one of the blessings of embracing exile in our current context is that it might help the church rediscover what it means to live as a unique group of people connected to God and to one another.

But if I can return to the hermeneutical circle chart for just a moment, I want to share one piece of good news with you before we move on. If you were to draw a line across the chart from three o'clock to nine o'clock—from Land to Division—you can see that the "best of times" for Israel happened above the line and the "worst of times" occurred below the line. If given the option, most sane people would want to live in the times above the line.

If my sense is correct, however, that we are in a time that has more commonalities with Israel's life below that line than above it, then this would not seem like very good news. As I have worked on these materials over the years, I have often complained to God that I would have preferred he had placed me in a time when the church was clearly in charge of the shaping of culture, a time when clergy were among the most respected people in the culture, and a time when the future of ministry seemed quite secure. No one goes skipping and whistling into exile.

But here is the great and glorious news. When you consider the Scriptures, the people of God seem to be at their best in the times below the line on the chart. When the people of God are secure and in power, they are not at their best. (Think about all the immoral judges, deceptive priests, and idolatrous kings). But when the people of God are in places of marginalization and need, they seem to allow the Spirit of God to dwell in them and empower them to live faithfully despite the challenges.

My hope is that embracing exile will actually be a source of hope and not despair. I'm convinced that exile is where God does his most transformative work in his people. My expectation, or even my goal, is not that this study might make modern-day Christians more optimistic and less pessimistic about the future. Optimism and pessimism are attitudes that come and go with the flow of world events and cultural swings. My desire is that this study might help the church of today become what the prophet Zechariah called "prisoners of hope" (Zech. 9:12, NRSV).

> Rejoice greatly, O daughter Zion!
> Shout aloud, O daughter Jerusalem!
> . . . .
> Return to your stronghold, O prisoners of hope;
> . . . .
> On that day the LORD their God will save them
> for they are the flock of his people;
> for like the jewels of a crown
> they shall shine on his land. (Vv. 9, 12, 16, NRSV)

Questions for Discussion

- In what ways does the metaphor of exile speak to you and help you make sense of the church and the surrounding culture?

- Do you think the church in your location has had its 587 BC moment? If so, what moment or moments embody 587 BC to you?

- Can you think of ways or times in the Bible when the people of God were at their best in exile?

- In what ways do you think a feeling or sense of exile in this time might be helpful for the church? Or in what ways might the feeling of exile help the church recover its uniqueness?

NOW YOU ARE GOD'S PEOPLE

"Thy kingdom come"—this is not the prayer of the pious soul of the
individual who wants to flee the world, nor is it the prayer of the
utopian and fanatic, the stubborn world reformer. Rather, this is
the prayer only of the church-community of children of the Earth
. . . who persevere together in the midst of the world, in its depths,
in the daily life and subjugation of the world.

—Dietrich Bonhoeffer, "Thy Kingdom Come!" Berlin, 1932

● ● ●

The most creative social strategy we have to offer is the church.
Here we show the world a manner of life the world can never
achieve through social coercion or governmental action.
We serve the world by showing it something that it is not, namely,
a place where God is forming a family out of strangers.

—Stanley Hauerwas and William Willimon, *Resident Aliens*

● ● ●

But you are a chosen race, a royal priesthood, a holy nation,
God's own people, in order that you may proclaim the mighty acts
of him who called you out of darkness into his marvelous light.

Once you were not a people,
but now you are God's people;
once you had not received mercy,
but now you have received mercy.
—1 Pet. 2:9-10, NRSV

● ● ●

Separation—Filling—Blessing

The Bible opens with these words: "In the beginning when God created the heavens and the earth, the earth was a formless void and darkness covered the face of the deep, while a wind from God swept over the face of the waters" (Gen. 1:1-2, NRSV). These first two verses in the Scriptures contain three of my favorite Hebrew words: *tohu*, *bohu*, and *ruach*.

Tohu and *bohu* are twin words that when they appear in the Bible always appear together. In Genesis 1:2 they are usually translated into English using words such as *formless* and *void*. But together they embody not just a lack of shape and empty space but in the Hebrew imagination all of the forces of chaos that can and often do break into life and turn things upside down. More often than not, *tohu* and *bohu* are symbolized by or take the form of water. That is certainly the form they take in the opening lines from the creation story. In the narrative this formlessness and this emptiness are embodied in darkness and the waters of the deep.

It is important to understand how ancient Hebrew people thought about large bodies of water. They didn't really like them. The Bible very often speaks of the oceans and seas as places of mystery, threat, fear, and chaos. Think about how many people in the

32

ancient world would have set out on voyages across the waters only to never return. Even in our own day massive floods and destructive tsunamis humble us. Or think about recent plane crashes or shipwrecks where these huge vessels—and the hundreds of people aboard them—have simply disappeared into the waters. I remember as a teenager a funeral at our church in Seattle for three fishermen whose boat went missing off the coast of Alaska, and no remnant of them or of their boat has ever been recovered.

If you can hold that chaotic and fearful picture of the "deep" in your mind, it might help you appreciate why the psalmist so often celebrates God's authority over the waters (see for example Ps. 29:3). Thinking about the watery image of *tohu* and *bohu* might give you a new perspective on the parting of the Red Sea in the Exodus story or on the texts in the Gospels where Jesus stills the storm or walks on the water. Having grown up mostly on the west coast of the United States and loving the Pacific Ocean, I have never been a fan of Revelation 21:1, where the Revelator envisions a "new heaven and a new earth; for the first heaven and the first earth had passed away, and *the sea was no more*" (NRSV, emphasis added). Now that I live five hundred miles from the nearest beach, I have been hoping God would make it up to me by offering me a beachfront mansion in the new creation. But apparently, in the eternal kingdom there is no more sea! However, if we think about the waters as the symbol of these ancient twins of chaos—*tohu* and *bohu*—we see clearly that what Revelation envisions is not a landlocked heaven but a new heaven and a new earth where all of the places of chaos and threat have been removed. The *tohu* and *bohu* have been defeated once and for all.

This leads me to my other favorite Hebrew word from the hymn of creation: *ruach*. *Ruach* is a word that means breath, wind, or spirit. In the beginning things were dominated by formlessness and emptiness, but the breath, the wind, or the Spirit of God hovered over the face of the waters of chaos.

Sometimes I invite my young students to think of Genesis 1 as the narration of a cosmic WWE (World Wrestling Entertainment) match. Imagine the microphone descending from the rafters and the announcer taking it and shouting, "Ladies and Gentlemen, it's the beginning! Let's get ready to rumble! In this corner are the reigning champions—the twins of chaos and destruction. They are formless. They are void. They are *Tohu* and *Bohu*!" At this point I imagine them as huge, steroid-enhanced wrestlers wearing tights and capes and scary Mexican wrestling masks. When they are announced, they taunt and jeer at the crowd while the spectators throw popcorn at them.

Then the announcer cries out, "And in this corner, we have the Challenger. He's omnipotent. He's omniscient. He's omnipresent. Every knee bow down and worship him! He's Yahweh!" At this point the crowd can't see anything, but a huge gust of wind sweeps across the spectators as they stand silently in awe and wonder.

What then ensues is a seven-round wrestling match in which God Almighty forms something out of nothing, and in a great act of love and power he speaks the universe into being and defeats the two great twins of chaos.

I'm obviously having some imaginative fun with the story, but let's get to the important point. What I find significant is how God creates, how he defeats the chaos.

In this great seven-verse hymn of creation God begins on day one by *separating* the light and the darkness (Gen. 1:3-5). The light he called day, and the darkness gets called night.

On the second day God places a dome in the midst of the waters and uses that dome to *separate* the waters. He places waters above the dome and calls those waters the sky. He then leaves waters below the dome, which remain as the seas (vv. 6-8).

On day three the dry land appears. The text, however, literally says that "God *separated* the waters into one place, and the dry land appeared" (v. 9, emphasis added; see vv. 9-13). (Most English translations say that God "gathered together," because it doesn't make sense in English for things to be separated together.)

I want you to notice two things. First, the opening three days are an attack on the *tohu*—on the formlessness. At the end of three days creation is formed with light and dark, sea and sky, and dry land. But I especially want you notice, second, that the primary verb is the same on the first three days of creation: *separation*. God separates light and dark, separates sea and sky, and separates out the dry land.

On days four, five, and six God takes on the *bohu*—the emptiness. On day four God *fills* the dark and light with the sun, the moon, and the stars (vv. 14-19). The fifth day brings about God's creation of birds to *fill* the sky and fish to *fill* the seas (vv. 20-23). Then on the sixth day God *fills* the earth with all sorts of animals and with humankind—made uniquely in God's image—as the crown of creation (vv. 24-31).

This time I want you to notice three things. First, God uses the second set of three days to take on and defeat the *bohu*. The emptiness is now filled. When evening and morning came at the end of the sixth day, the twins of chaos—formlessness and emptiness—had been eliminated. Second, I want you to notice the relationship between the days. What God formed on day one (light and dark) is filled on day four (with sun, moon, and stars). What God formed on day two (sea and sky) is filled on day five (with birds and fish). And what God formed on day three (dry land) is filled on day six (with animals and humans). How cool is that, by the way? That sound you hear is your mind blowing!

Finally, and most importantly, what I want you to notice is the key verb for days four through six. The key word is *filling*. The first three days are divine acts of *separation*. The second three days are divine acts of *filling*.

But there is of course a seventh day: a day of rest, a day of peace. To go back to my WWE illustration, it's as though the bell rings for the final round and the *tohu* and *bohu* have been knocked out. The Spirit of God controlled the waters, and out of them creation emerged. The final day was therefore a day of *blessing*. "So God blessed the seventh day and hallowed it" (2:3, NRSV).

If you are still with me, what I want you to capture are the three key verbs from the opening creation account: *separation*, *filling*, and *blessing*. Write them down on a sticky note somewhere. Make a refrigerator magnet out of them.

Here is a chart to help you picture how these three key words—*separation*, *filling*, and *blessing*—fit into the Bible's opening chapters:

TOHU—FORMLESS	*BOHU*—VOID
Day 1: **SEPARATION** of Light and Dark	Day 4: **FILLING** with Sun, Moon, and Stars
Day 2: **SEPARATION** of Sea and Sky	Day 5: **FILLING** with Birds and Fish
Day 3: **SEPARATION** of Dry Land	Day 6: **FILLING** with Animals and Humans
Day 7: **BLESSING**	

That's Cool . . . but Who Cares?

So, big deal! Why is it important to notice these three words: *separation*, *filling*, and *blessing*? Maybe it would help to ask this question: Why would the people of God want to tell the story of creation in this particular way to their children? I am, by the way, making some important assumptions with that question. I am assuming that the point of the Bible's opening chapter goes beyond just relaying information about *how* creation took place. Perhaps more importantly it is informing us *why* creation happened and most significantly *what kind of people* we should be in light of the way God created. If the Scripture was written, read, and kept by God's people in order to help form the next generations of faithful followers, then the form or pattern of the story is critical (especially for people who were oral learners).

I am convinced that the opening chapter of Genesis comes to the people of God in this pattern because they wanted their children to interpret the world God created through the three words of *separation*, *filling*, and *blessing*.

Notice, by the way, that one of the next critical scriptural stories follows a very similar pattern. God asks Abram and Sarai (later known as Abraham and Sarah) to *separate* themselves from their places of protection and provision. If they will do that, God in turn promises to *fill* their lives with his presence. And out of that covenant relationship between God and his people the whole world will be *blessed* (Gen. 12:1-3).

Before you call all of your neighbors to tell them how cool that is, let me back up a minute. When we left the opening hymn of creation, the *tohu* and *bohu* had been defeated. But one way to read the narrative of the garden of Eden (in Gen. 2 and 3) and humankind's descent into sin is to read it as the reawakening of the chaos. It is as though Adam and Eve's rebellion against God's purposes gives life back to the chaos God's Spirit had put at bay. One of the other important symbols of *tohu* and *bohu* is not only water but also violence. Once the forces of chaos and sin are reawakened in Eden, we should not be surprised that in the second generation of Genesis, one brother turns and kills the other. The violence and chaos of Cain builds right into the Noah story where God's heart is grieved because "the earth was corrupt in God's sight, and the earth was filled with violence" (6:11, NRSV).

If I have your imagination now thoroughly shaped by *tohu* and *bohu*, the story of the flood and the deliverance of Noah and his family should also take on new meaning. When the flood of God's judgment begins in Genesis 7:11, the waters actually spring up from the ground first. It is as though the waters God separated on day three break back over the dry land. Then the text literally says, "And God opened the windows in the dome of the sky" (v. 11). It is as though God went around and rolled down all the windows in the great dome that was used on day two to separate the sea and the sky. The text pictures God removing all the boundaries he had used to separate the waters of chaos, and the *tohu* and *bohu* come crashing back down upon creation. Thus the story of Noah is not just a scary flood story but a story about the world reverting back to its original formless and empty chaos.

But how does God redeem the world after the flood? His *ruach*—his breath—blows across the waters again (8:1-3), and the waters return to where they are supposed to be. The righteous remnant of Noah and his family become the instrument through which God's re-creation begins. In an important sense, Noah and his family also experience the separation, filling, and blessing of God. Do you see it?

Now let's bring the story of Abram and Sarai back into the picture. If we include it along with the other two key Genesis stories, we begin to see clearly that separating, filling, and blessing is not just the pattern through which God created originally but *also the pattern through which God brings about and will continue to bring about his new creation*. This is why I think Israel told these stories to their children with this pattern in mind. The people of God wanted their children to understand that the same way God formed creation in the beginning—separation, filling, and blessing—is the same way that he is still bringing about the redemption of creation. *God is separating out a unique people in the world. He is filling them with his Spirit. And through them the world will be blessed.*

It is fascinating to see how this pattern continues to have significance not only throughout the rest of the Old Testament but into the New Testament concept of the church or the body of Christ as well. The Greek word that is translated "church"—*ekklēsia*—literally means the "called-out ones." The New Testament church came into existence as a group of both Jews and Gentiles who were called out—*separated*—from the world, and then, like the apostles at Pentecost, were *filled* by the Spirit in order to be sent out as a redemptive *blessing* to the world.

So What's the Problem?

That was so much fun! Now let me summarize what I am trying to say. I am convinced that from the beginning God has, in his love and by his Spirit, been defeating the powers of chaos and sin. However, the primary way he has done this (and continues to do this) is by *separating* out a people, *filling* them with his presence, and making them a *blessing* to the world. This was true in the Old Testament era with Israel—God's unique nation. This was true in the New Testament era with a people called the church or the body of Christ. And the Revelator sees this as true into the future as God forms a people, not marked by the beastly ways of Babylon, but reflecting the light and life of the Lamb who was slain.

Everyone say, "Amen!"

So what's the problem? The problem is that most of us—although we hopefully say "amen" to the statements above—have not really been shaped to believe or to imagine the gospel in those terms. Most contemporary Christians, especially in Western cultures, are so steeped in forms of individualism that they don't really think of the church as people to whom they belong. Somewhere along the line historically the church thought less about being a uniquely "called-out" or separated people in the world who reflect the character and nature of God to others and more about being a helping institution whose primary purpose is to make sure individual Christians are happy in this life and get to heaven in the next.

Please don't misunderstand me. It's not that having an assurance of eternal life is unimportant. It certainly is. But in the Scriptures, eternal life is a gift given to the people who make up Christ's body—his "chosen race," his "royal priesthood," his "holy nation" (1 Pet. 2:9, NRSV). The Great Commission is not a call to go out and get individuals into heaven. The commission of Christ to his disciples is a call to invite people through baptism (we'll come back to this in more detail later) to enter into the people who bear the name of the Father, Son, and Holy Spirit upon their community.

There are likely many reasons why the church has lost a sense of being a unique people in the world.

Part of it happened quite naturally in the West when around AD 325 the Roman emperor Constantine gave Christianity a favored place in the Roman world. In a short span of time the Christian faith moved from its exiled Jewish and persecuted apostolic roots and started running the empire. This is certainly not all bad. The end of Christian persecution is something the people of God rightly celebrated. Having Christians serving in positions of authority often (but not always) helped to form more just, equitable, and peaceful systems of government. But it also had its drawbacks. Christians were no longer persecuted. But sometimes they became the new persecutors. The church at times ceased to be a unique "nation" of people that transcends every boundary, language, and custom and became associated with particular historical nations. There is a significant dynamic of faith lost when one becomes a "Christian" simply by being a citizen of a particular "Christian nation."

In Europe and America this "Constantinian" impulse was matched with the rise of individualism during the Enlightenment. Again, individualism is in many ways a wonderful thing. In particular the elevation of the rights of persons for self-determination is a great gift to people. Individual freedom is a value rightly celebrated and guarded. But a few centuries into the Enlightenment the downsides of "rugged individualism" are easy to see. Individualism ends up isolating people from one another. A culture shaped by individualism usually forms people who are self-centered. People who only know how to speak and think in patterns of individualism cannot sustain commitments that no longer "work for them" or make them feel good.

If we take the Constantinian impulse, add in individualism, and then just for fun mix in the technological age's love of consumerism, the blend becomes deadly for the church's ecclesiology. Again, there are many good things about living in a culture where people have lots of choices. Every person does have to consume some things—like food and water—to live. A world where people have a range of options to choose from is a blessing. But a world where everything becomes a self-centered choice and even relationships become one more thing to consume is scary.

What seems to have happened in the last few decades is the church has ceased for many people to be a people into whom we have been baptized or a body into whom we have been engrafted. Rather, the church is a place individual citizens of a particular culture come to consume the things of Jesus offered to them in order to make their lives work better or to help them feel better about their lives. The church has become a place we go to consume the things of Jesus ("to be fed") and not a community of resident-alien disciples to whom we have been covenanted.

By the way, I am convinced this is why those who pursue a call into ministry find themselves increasingly entering into a career path prone to burnout and detrimental to mental and physical health. Most people pursue the call to ministry believing they are going to get a chance to lead a holy people. What they discover is that they have become the manager of a department store selling the goods of Jesus to highly discriminating shoppers. Leading a people isn't easy (see Moses), but it's cake compared to running a superstore for Christ hoping people don't get tired of your "product" and start shopping for their spiritual goods elsewhere.

In this sense, perhaps embracing exile may be wonderful for the church.

If Constantinianism—the church's impulse to run the empire—is dead (or at least dying), perhaps that frees up the church to become a unique people witnessing to a countercultural way of life. It's hard to run the empire without eventually looking and acting like it.

Perhaps a people who are tired of the isolation of rugged individualism and who are devastated by commitments that can't be sustained will rediscover that they were created by God for community and seek a community of people that invites them to find their lives through self-sacrifice and covenant.

And maybe, just maybe, there are a few folks out there who will get tired of the selfish kind of people consumerism forms them to be. And they will discover a hunger and a thirst for the world to be set right. They will hear a call to separate themselves from the self-centeredness and carnality of the world. They will be filled with the unique self-emptying Spirit of Christ. And they will seek together to be a blessing to the world.

Again, exile may help us rediscover the church as "a chosen race, a royal priesthood, a holy nation" (1 Pet. 2:9, NRSV). Once we lost our identity as a people, but now God can form us again as his countercultural people.

A people who desire to live as a community of covenant need two things to survive and thrive. They need a life-giving story, and they need sustaining practices. Let's turn to those two things in the next chapters.

Questions for Discussion

- How do the terms *separation*, *filling*, and *blessing* shape your imagination? Why do you think that pattern is so important and so frequent in the Bible?

- What do you think separation looks like for the people of God where you are located?

- What are ways that you think the filled people of God can be a blessing to the world?

- What do you think it would take in this consumer-oriented age for people to think of the church not just as a place they go to get help or to consume the "things of Jesus" but also as something God is forming his people into for the sake of the world?

3
THIS IS MY STORY

The New Testament is not a text to be analyzed so much as a set of scripts for forming a company of performers, a movement that will be Christianity.

—Terrence Tilley, *The Disciples' Jesus*

● ● ●

I can only answer the question "What am I to do?" if I can answer the prior question "Of what story or stories do I find myself a part?"

—Alasdair MacIntyre, *After Virtue*

● ● ●

By faith we understand that the worlds were prepared by the word of God, so that what is seen was made from things that are not visible.

—Heb. 11:3, NRSV

● ● ●

Philosophers have begun to recognize the need all people have for a story that makes sense out of life. In fact, it may be impossible to live life without a story.

A life story or narrative (what also might be called a *worldview*) is necessary in order to answer several important life questions: Where am I or what kind of world is this? Who am I or what does it mean to be a person? What time is it or what is the nature of the world right now? What's the problem? And if there is a problem, what's the solution?

One of the ways to think about the increasing sense of exile that many Christians feel is to think about it as a loss or marginalization of the biblical story as the primary shared cultural story (what might be called a *metanarrative*).

Let's go back to Constantine in AD 325. After he made Christianity the favored religion in Rome, the story of the Christian faith increasingly shaped the imagination of people throughout the Roman Empire, even if some people weren't devoted to Christ. For a millennium or more in the West the biblical story shaped the way most people thought about marriage, politics, nature, work, and even death. Even if a person never attended a church service, it is highly likely that the Christian story had so saturated the culture that it informed the way that person interpreted the world. People married one another shaped by the imagination of God's covenant with his people. Monarchs ruled nations with authority people believed had been ordained by God. The laws of nature were a reflection of the will of the Creator. Work was viewed as an opportunity to fulfill the purposes and gifts given to each person by divine providence. And one's future after death was determined by the judgments of the holy and righteous God.

Even if a person decided to live in rejection of that "Christian story," it was still the dominant cultural narrative of faith that defined that person's rebellion.

Sometime in the early seventeenth century things began to change. I blame (or credit) the invention of the telescope (1608) added to the earlier invention of the printing press (1440). With the telescope Galileo and other astronomers began to more accurately chart the movement of the heavenly bodies. Earlier, Copernicus (d. 1543) had hypothesized that the long-held assumption (and teaching of the church) that the universe revolves around the earth was false. Now, Galileo, supporting Copernicus, validated through observation that the universe is not geocentric but heliocentric. Humankind is not actually seated in the center of all things, but we are instead floating around on the third rock from the sun!

On the list of potential things for the church to be wrong about, the location of the earth in the universe is pretty big. In fear and frustration, there was an attempt made by the religious authorities to force Galileo to recant. But in a world with printing presses, secrets are hard to keep.

It is a gross oversimplification, but in some sense what historians have labeled the Renaissance and the Enlightenment occurred in response to the realization that if the dominant cultural story of faith has been wrong about the location of the earth, what else is that story wrong about?

Prior to the Enlightenment, we might think of the story that shaped the average person's thoughts in the following way:

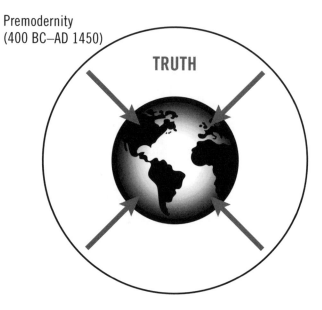

Premodernity
(400 BC–AD 1450)

For the pre-Enlightenment or premodern mind, everything that is seen around us is or was formed by forces outside of what we see or experience materially. This was not just true for the Christian story. In the pre-Constantinian era most cultures had metanarratives about various deities and how all that exists is a reflection of their creative work. Even Plato reasoned that everyting that is seen in the material world is simply a reflection of the forms or ideas that exist in the "spiritual" realm of pure being. For Plato, concepts such as justice and love are known in the material world (or the realm of becoming) because they are reflections of the form or ideas of justice and love in the realm of being. For Plato, and for the Christian story, in order to understand what is happening in the visible world, one must have a good understanding of the invisible world.

What happened during the Enlightenment—in a period sometimes called *modernity*—was that although most people did not doubt that there were forces beyond the material world that shaped the visible world, they began to seriously wonder if people knew clearly the true nature of those forces. To quote from the *X-Files*, people knew the "truth is out there."[1] They just weren't convinced that the Truth (with a capital *T*) was fully known. Scientists and philosophers began to throw off their previous assumptions, got rid of the old stories, and tried to start over with a blank slate to discover the mind of God. The quest for truth in the modern period looks more like this:

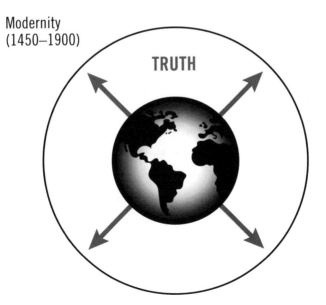

Modernity
(1450–1900)

TRUTH

An interesting thing happened as scholars and scientists stopped reasoning from the outside in and started working from the inside out. Small things that were viewed as the building blocks of the world became more interesting than the big things. What the world had assumed about God and heaven seemed much less interesting—and far less certain—than what people were discovering about atoms and matter. By the time the Enlightenment was in full swing, theologians had been mostly displaced in universities. The high-paid faculty members were now the physicists. Martin Luther's picture on the college brochure was replaced with Albert Einstein's.

Let me be the first to say that a lot of wonderful things happened when "modern" people started throwing off everything they assumed to be true during the "premodern" period. Huge leaps forward were made (and continue to be made) in science, technology, and medicine. Many monarchies and other forms of oppressive governments were replaced with developing systems of democracy. Pursuing reason unencumbered by previously held assumptions has done some tremendous things for the world.

One area, however, where freedom from the older stories, narratives, and assumptions was not as life giving was ethics. But for a while no one really noticed. Because the imaginations of most Western cultures were so deeply shaped by centuries of Christianity, it took awhile for people to notice things were changing. For example, many of the founding fathers of America were openly deistic. Although leaders such as Jefferson, Madison, and Hamilton rejected the biblical accounts of miracles and seriously doubted that God interacts daily in the world, they still hung on to God's order and much of the Bible's sense of moral law.

But eventually things did begin to change. It may seem strange in a book about living biblically to discuss one of the world's most famous atheists, but let me share two stories from the wild and crazy philosopher Friedrich Nietzsche to illustrate where things started to come unhinged.

Nietzsche (1844–1900) began to recognize that although the intellectual world had largely thrown off the religious narratives that had formed a millennium of Western culture, the moral codes of that tradition still shaped the imaginations and the lifestyles of most people. In his view, the old moral narratives had been pushed aside but they still were telling people what to do. He saw this as an attempt by the leaders in the culture to manipulate people, and so he called it a "will to power."

In response he invited people to imagine a great fire-breathing dragon from which people were living in fear. Scales cover the dragon, and on each scale are written two words: "Thou shalt!" This dragon is Nietzsche's representation of the old moral (primarily Christian) story still telling people what they shall and shall not do. He then imagined humankind as having the power to overcome the dragon, for in the hand of every person is a sword inscribed with two other words: "I will!" The duty of thoughtful people, argued Nietzsche, is to find every possible way to overcome the moral system's attempts to will its power. Every "overcomer" (whom Nietzsche labeled *übermensch* or "superhuman") should slay the dragon of "Thou shalt!" with the sword of "I will!"[2] Sociologists often refer to those "Thou shalts" as *social constructions*.

I know that sounds strange. But think about the various ways over the last century culture has celebrated, become fascinated with, and has been deeply shaped by cultural figures who took on and destroyed (or deconstructed) various social constructions.

Some of those overcomers have done wonderful things. For example, Dr. Martin Luther King Jr. is rightly celebrated as one who deconstructed many of the social constructions of racism in America. The dragon of racism was covered in scales that said, "Thou shalt sit at the back of the bus." "Thou shalt not have an equal vote." "Thou shalt be segregated from the white population." And "Thou shalt not receive the same opportunities to flourish and succeed." Dr. King rightly invited people to join him in forms of peaceful protest and take up the sword of "I will" and slay that dragon of oppression.

But there have been many other social constructions and social norms that have been deconstructed by various people across the last century that have probably not been so good for the culture. Let me give you some basic examples from the last century:

- The increased use and acceptance of profanity.
- The proliferation of pornography and sexual imagery.
- The viewing of increasingly graphic depictions of violence.
- The acceptance of unmarried cohabitation, sexual promiscuity, and the redefinition of marriage.

In each of these cases it would be easy to list cultural movements or cultural icons that drew attention to the lines of social construction in a particular area and then proceeded either to eliminate those lines or to find ways to move them. Let me give you an example of someone who took the sword of "I will" in order to slay the dragon of "Thou shalt" in the use of profanity. The late comedian George Carlin became well known for a stand-up routine he called "7 Words You Can't Say on TV." Over a six-minute period Carlin not only continuously repeated the seven words banned by the FCC (Federal Communications Commission) as too profane for television but in doing so also proceeded to demonstrate how somewhat arbitrary he thought the choice to ban those seven particular words was. In a very Nietzschean way, only six minutes were needed for Carlin to deconstruct the ban on those seven words as a "will to power" by people in control of the broadcasting system.

What the FCC had declared profane, George Carlin proclaimed humorous.

What the Victorian era had defined as "proper," Hugh Hefner decreed as repressive.

What the Motion Picture Association determined to be too graphic, Martin Scorsese deemed to be art.

And what the history of Western civilization had historically defined as marriage was ruled to be no more than an unjust limitation of civil rights by a portion of the religious population.

For a century now there have been dead dragons everywhere. Again, not all of this has been bad. Some dragons—like socially constructed forms of racism and sexism—needed to die; they deserved to be deconstructed. But in this new period that some philosophers have called *postmodernity* every metanarrative, every story that held the moral life together and gave meaning to people's actions, has likely been deconstructed by someone. If we were to illustrate this postmodern mind-set, it might look something like this:

Postmodernity
(1900–____)

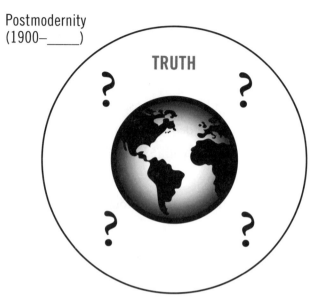

In modernity, the older stories, the dominant metanarratives, were thrown off as people pursued the truth they were convinced was out there. In postmodernity, a level of uncertainty seeped into the hearts of many people causing them to wonder if there is indeed anything called truth that a person might discover. If it is indeed the case that truth is not out there, then the only alternative is for moral truth to be whatever the individual thinks it ought to be. Not surprisingly *Oxford English Dictionary*'s word of the year for 2016 was *post-truth*. The fear for many philosophers is that in a postmodern world "truth is what your contemporaries let you get away with."[3]

Although Nietzsche found the slaying of social constructions and defeating various "wills to power" quite invigorating, there is another side to him that I would like to point out. In his work *Thus Spoke Zarathustra*, Nietzsche imagines a kind of postmodern prophet who goes from town to town declaring the death of God. "'Whither is God [?]' [the madman] cried. 'I shall tell you. *We have killed him*—you and I. All of us are his murderers. . . . What did we do when we unchained this earth from its sun?'"[4] But no one in the town listens or pays attention to this seemingly crazy prophet because they are too busy being entertained to notice.

When Nietzsche—in his atheism—proclaimed the death of God, he did not mean that God was once alive but has now expired in old age. What he meant is that the story of a God who formed all things and gave meaning to creation is no longer the story that shapes the culture. For Nietzsche, when the Enlightenment eliminated the metanarrative of faith, it essentially killed the idea of God. But now this is no longer a message of good news inviting people to go slay all of the dragons of "Thou shalt." It is rather a message of despair that the "earth has been unchained from the sun." In the end for Nietzsche, once God is dead, life has no more meaning. Without God there is no more certainty or hope about the future. When the only meaning life has is the meaning an individual creates, it ceases to have any real or lasting significance. When the story that gave people meaning and purpose—the story of God—is gone, all that remains is a kind of hopeless despair.

I have taken you on this odd journey to come back to this simple point. People can't live without a story. Nietzsche, by the way, is not without a story. His story, like the story for many in this postmodern era, is that there is no story (which oddly is still a kind of story). But as I've tried to demonstrate, believing there is no overarching story can be exciting because it gives a person the freedom to write his or her own story. However, if there is no larger story into which our individual stories fit, life ends up quite empty and our self-written stories end up looking and feeling quite shallow.

Where Do People without a Story Go?

There are alternatives to living without a story. As the Christian story began to decline in influence, other stories emerged to vie for people's devotion.

There is the *success story*, in which life is about accumulating wealth, power, and pleasurable experiences. This story's primary slogan is, "Whoever dies with the most toys wins!"

A lot of people have lived into the *nation story*. In the nation story people find their primary identity within a certain culture, race, or language. The things that matter most in that story are the wealth, power, expansion, and stability of one's nation. That story has been quite persuasive over the last couple of centuries. Many people have lived and died embracing that story.

The *humanist story* has also become quite pervasive. This story's plot says that the point of life is to keep helping humanity become better. There is much to admire in this story. But in the end when the humanity story isn't part of a larger narrative of meaning, it, too, usually ends up in some form of Nietzschean despair.

Another possibility is that people *live out many stories at once.* Philosopher Alasdair MacIntyre is convinced that most people live out their morality today using fragments from a number of different narratives.

While I was in seminary, my wife, Debbie, worked at Warner Bros. and many of our friends were connected to the television and film industry. Two of our dear friends—I'll call them Doug and

Rachel—were television writers and close friends with Debbie. In addition to work, Debbie and Rachel were both pregnant at the same time. We would often go to dinner and talk Hollywood and baby furniture. Neither Doug nor Rachel professed to be Christian, but we nevertheless grew to become good friends.

One night at dinner Debbie and the two friends were talking about people who were getting advanced at the studio. In particular they were unhappy about a person who had the reputation for being quite deceitful and ruthless and who had just been given a significant promotion. In the midst of their complaining Doug commented, "I wish that I could lie and backstab people. I'm sure I would be much more successful today if I could be more ruthless, but I just can't."

In the midst of their conversation, Rachel looked at me and said, "Scott, as a pastor and an ethicist, this conversation about the underside of the 'industry' has to be driving you crazy."

"No," I responded. "It is actually quite interesting. But I do have a question for you, Doug. Earlier you said you would be much more successful if you could cheat, lie, and backstab your way to the top. If that's the case, I'm curious why you don't do just that? Why don't you cheat your way to the top?"

He looked at me with a great deal of exasperation. "I can't believe my one pastor friend, and the only person I know getting a doctorate in ethics, would ask me that kind of question!"

"Wait," I replied. "I know why I can't do those things. I have a whole bunch of reasons why I wouldn't cheat my way to success. But you don't share any of my faith convictions. I know why I couldn't do it. I'm just curious to know why you can't do it."

My question ruined the rest of dinner for Doug. I could see him wrestling with the problem all the way through dessert. Just as we were about to leave, Doug interjected, "All right, Daniels! I know why I can't cheat and backstab. My grandmother was a very good Catholic. And every time I'm in a situation where I am tempted to lie or cheat, it's like the ghost of my grandmother pops up on my shoulder and whispers, 'Doug . . . don't do that.'"

On the way home Debbie laughed and remarked, "It was funny to watch you catch Doug with that question tonight. Isn't it interesting that he feels like much of his moral compass comes from his grandmother's Catholic faith?"

"Yes," I replied. "But the question I didn't have the heart to ask was, 'What will be the reason their new child will give someday for not cheating his or her way to the top?'"

The point of the story is not that Doug and Rachel are bad people. They are actually very fine people. But my sense is that the story that shapes and informs their moral life—like most people— is a complicated patchwork of religious fragments, citizenship fragments, success fragments, humanism fragments, and lots of other pieces. But it is very hard to live well out of a fragmented story. And it is very difficult to pass on a fragmented story that will guide the next generation. People living in exile have to have a coherent and cohesive story.

A Storied People

In a world without a coherent story, the church exists as a people who not only tell but also live into and out of a truthful story. The people of God in exile know that what they need is to come each week to submit their lives to the authority of the Scriptures' story and to be formed again and again to live out that story in the world.

I love the eleventh chapter of Hebrews—the "by faith" chapter. The beauty of this chapter is certainly found in the recounting of the great lives of trust lived out by our ancestors in the faith. But I also love the way the chapter begins. "By faith *we* understand that the worlds were prepared by the word of God, so that what is seen was made from things that are not visible" (v. 3, NRSV). The emphasis on the word *we* is mine. By faith the church (the "we" in this text) understands and accepts this story of God as true and beautiful and good. Not everyone has embraced God's great story. In fact the majority of the culture around the church may be living out of very different stories than the story of faith. But this is our story. It is the church's story. "By faith *we* understand . . ."

To be a storied people is to live the story. I love an illustration given by Bishop N. T. Wright in a paper he presented on the authority of the Scriptures. He writes,

Suppose there exists a Shakespeare play whose fifth act had been lost. The first four acts provide, let us suppose, such a wealth of characterization, such a crescendo of excitement within the plot, that it is generally agreed that the play ought to be staged. Nevertheless, it is felt inappropriate actually to write a fifth act once and for all: it would freeze the play into one form, and commit Shakespeare as it were to being prospectively responsible for work not in fact his own. Better, it might be felt, to give the key parts to highly trained, sensitive and experienced Shakespearian actors, who would immerse themselves in the first four acts, and in the language and culture of Shakespeare and his time, and *who would then be told to work out a fifth act for themselves.*[5]

What a beautiful picture of what it means to be a storied people. For Wright, the first four acts of the divine drama are "(1) Creation," "(2) Fall," "(3) Israel," "(4) Jesus," and the missing fifth act is the church.[6] His powerful illustration invites the church to so immerse itself in God's saving story in acts 1 through 4 that the faithful then know how to live authentically in ways that carry the great story forward.

If I could make one adjustment to Wright's illustration, it would be that I think the Scriptures point in hazy yet profound ways to what the great sixth act—we might call it eschaton or eternity—will look like. The storied people of the church dwell so fully in the first four acts, and their imaginations have been so shaped by the story of Christ's resurrection power and the Spirit's healing of creation, that now in act 5 the church lives as faithful witnesses to God's great story.

> *This is my story, this is my song,*
> *Praising my Savior all the day long;*
> *This is my story, this is my song,*
> *Praising my Savior all the day long.*[7]

Questions for Discussion

- If you could summarize the story you think most people in the culture live out in their daily lives, how would you describe that story?

- What do you think about the idea that most people live out of fragments or pieces of many stories at once?

- What story fragments do you think sneak into and perhaps corrupt the church's ability to live God's story faithfully?

- What do you think of N. T. Wright's Shakespeare example? How might thinking of the nature of the Scriptures in this way shape the way the church reads Scripture?

HOLINESS TAKES PRACTICE(S)

My practices aren't designed for your enjoyment.
—Coach Norman Dale to basketball player, *Hoosiers*

● ● ●

Liturgies aim our love to different ends precisely by training our hearts through our bodies.
—James K. A. Smith, *Desiring the Kingdom*

● ● ●

Do not be conformed to this world, but be transformed by the renewing of your minds, so that you may discern what is the will of God—what is good and acceptable and perfect.
—Rom. 12:2, NRSV

● ● ●

There is a parable credited to Søren Kierkegaard about a town of ducks. These ducks for decades had waddled everywhere they went. In the mornings they waddled to work and to school. In the evenings they waddled back home. Every Sunday the ducks waddled to church. Each week the duck pastor would open the duck bible and preach about how God had given ducks the gift of wings with which they could soar above the earth and see the world from a different perspective. This sermon would always bless the ducks, and they would all quack their amens. Then the ducks would stand up and waddle home.[1]

My version of the duck parable happened several years ago when I was preaching a revival using the Sermon on the Mount in a little church in Arkansas. It was one of those wonderful, loving country churches where the people are warm and responsive to the message. There were several folks throughout the week who would say "Amen" or "Hallelujah" or even "Keep preaching!" during the message. That was all I needed! They helped me preach with everything I had to give.

I saved my favorite parts of the Sermon on the Mount—all of the peacemaking, forgiving, and loving-your-enemies sections—for the concluding service on Sunday morning. The sermon could not have gone any better. The congregation was alive and responsive. I was on fire. Heaven and earth touched. Many people responded to an invitation to come and pray at the altar. I closed the service convinced that the spirit of revival had indeed come to that little corner of the Ozarks.

After the benediction I went just a few steps down the hall from the sanctuary to the nursery to pick up our oldest son, Caleb—who was probably three or four at the time. I asked the nursery attendant how the morning had gone for him. She responded, "Oh, Caleb is such a sweet boy. He's done so well this week. Well . . . , we did have one little problem today. There was a new little boy who kept hitting the others. So I told Caleb, if he hits you again, you just hit him back."

I smiled and said, "You don't get to hear the sermons in here, do you?"

She laughed and replied, "Oh, yes we do. And I thought the message today was just what we needed."

Her answer amused me but didn't surprise me. Sometimes I think I can see written above the doors at the rear of every sanctuary these words: "That was nice, pastor. But now as we go back into the 'real world'. . ." I'm not surprised that any person shaped day after day by the fears and violence that pervade the culture would instinctively respond to being hit with immediately hitting back. I was just shocked that morning that I only had to walk about a hundred feet from the sanctuary to be back in the "real world."

What the church needs are not just more sermons telling the stories about the reconciling nature of the cross, the call by Jesus for disciples to love their enemies, and reminders that peacemakers are the blessed children in God's kingdom. We do need to constantly be reminded that our story is a one of overcoming the evil in the world with good. But what the church also needs are practices of reconciliation and forgiveness that rehabituate the lives of the faithful into people who might actually go into the world and turn the other cheek or go the second mile. In other words, until the ducks practice flying, they will simply keep waddling home.

Cultural Liturgies and Counterliturgies

Someone who has helped me come to appreciate the formative power of practices more deeply is my friend James K. A. Smith in his books *Desiring the Kingdom: Worship, Worldview, and Cultural Formation* and *You Are What You Love: The Spiritual Power of Habit*. Going back to the great work of Augustine of Hippo, Smith argues that humans are primarily driven by what they desire—what they love. According to Smith, the heart—the seat of desire—is shaped by various pictures of what we believe are most important, good, and true in our lives.

Jesus doesn't encounter Matthew and John—or you and me—and ask, "What do you know?" He doesn't even ask, "What do you believe?" He asks, "What do you want?" This is the most incisive, piercing question Jesus can ask of us precisely because we *are* what we want. Our wants and longings and desires are at the core of our identity, the wellspring from which our actions and behavior flow. Our wants reverberate from our heart, the epicenter of the human person. Thus Scripture counsels, "Above all else, guard your heart, for everything you do flows from it" (Prov. 4:23 [, NIV]). Discipleship, we might say, is a way to curate your heart, to be attentive to and intentional about what you love.

So discipleship is more a matter of hungering and thirsting than of knowing and believing.[2]

The incredible insight from Smith is not just that humans are driven by their desires but further that those desires are formed in us through various practices—Smith calls them "cultural liturgies." He labels them liturgies on purpose because they are for him forms of worship. Smith argues that almost every human activity has some kind of vision of the good life—a vision of what is ultimate and is worth loving most—built into the practice itself. Those practices then form our desires by teaching us to worship or make ultimate particular visions of the good life.

Think of cultural liturgies as rituals that habituate a person's life even when he or she is not aware of it. In certain areas of life we affirm repetitive rituals. At the beginning of this chapter I included a quote from Coach Norman Dale, played by Gene Hackman, in one of my all-time favorite sports movies, *Hoosiers*. Coach Dale inherits a ragtag, undisciplined Indiana basketball team from Hickory High. But after putting them through rigorous and repetitive drills and practices that instill the fundamentals of the game deep within their muscle memory, they turn into state champions. We recognize that pursuing excellence or mastery in just about any activity requires routines and disciplines that are formative precisely because they are repetitive.

If we are formed or habituated through repetitive rituals and practices, Smith wants us to imagine how much our desires are shaped through cultural liturgies such as shopping, advertising, entertainment, community events, and forms of education. He especially wants us to pay attention to the way these cultural liturgies deform or misinform our desires and thus the "kingdom" that we "seek first."

For example, Smith wants his readers to think of the local shopping mall not just as a place to purchase goods but also as a house of worship—as a kind of temple of consumption. The mall is not just a convenient place to buy things but also a place that is—through repetitive practices and images—portraying various pictures of the good life. At a level that is seldom noticed, the mall invites its "congregants" to give themselves for a vision of the good life embodied in a new pair of jeans, a new electronic gadget, or the right kind of furniture. For Smith, Americans are not great consumers by accident. It has taken a lot of practice(s).

If Smith is right that people are constantly being formed—whether they recognize it or not—by cultural liturgies, then Christian worship, in contrast, should be viewed as offering to people a set of counterformative practices that through repetition shape the hearts of the people of God to desire what is holy in order to pursue the kingdom of God.

Worship as Counterformation

In the last couple of decades many evangelical churches have had an increased interest in and a recovery of some of the ancient practices of Christian worship. While some evangelicals have been nervous that this interest in ancient practices of worship signals a dangerous return to pre-Reformation Christianity or indicates the influence on Christianity of odd forms of mysticism, my own sense is that there are a couple of reasons why many churches are rediscovering the formative wisdom and power of certain historic practices of the Christian faith and are thus discerning ways to reimagine ancient traditions in new contexts.

The first reason springs from a desire many people have to be rooted in something deeper than just the present. In a future chapter I will discuss the spiritual formation of young people in more detail. But for now, imagine being the average young person in today's world. Nearly half of all young people are being raised in broken homes with very little security or stability. For many who are several generations past their immigrant forebears, there is little or no connection to or even knowledge of a distinct cultural heritage. The world a young person has known has changed more rapidly than at any other time in human history. Very little has been permanent; almost everything has been disposable. For many young people, even the kinds of Christian communities they have experienced are denominationally independent, having arisen with little history, and dependent upon the gifts and charisma of one particular leader. It would be very natural, given those circumstances, that a generation would come along hungry for forms of Christian practice that might offer to them the stability, grounding, and permanence that is lacking in nearly every other part of their lives.

Second, I think there are many church leaders who are wondering if the kinds of practices that have most defined the contemporary church—practices directed toward meeting the consumeristic tendencies of people shaped by the cultural liturgies of the local shopping mall—have fulfilled the church's mission to make disciples of Jesus or if, as I mentioned earlier, those attractional practices of worship have simply formed fickle church shoppers and nitpicky Christian consumers.

The list of ancient worship practices and spiritual disciplines that might be recovered would be more exhaustive than I can give here. But let me suggest some practices that many in the evangelical world are recovering that ought to be considered seriously for their counterformative power in the body of Christ.

Some are rediscovering the formative power of keeping time with the seasons and rhythms of the church year. I often joke with college students who are excited about graduating that they have no idea what's going to happen to their body clocks over the next couple of years. For as long as they can remember, their internal clocks have been formed by the academic year. The year for them has started in mid-August or early September with the annual excursion to the superstore for school supplies, the mall for new clothes, and the local strip mall for a haircut. But after they are out of school, the rhythm of the academic calendar will be gone. When they have a "real" job, time will be pretty constant. A company may give them two weeks of vacation, but the remaining fifty weeks of the year will be just work. September will feel just like March. And July will be just like February.

In the Christian tradition, like its Jewish heritage, seasons of the year were used as opportunities to observe festivals and holidays. These moments of sacred time were set aside to remember and be formed by God's activity in the past in order to prepare for God's activity in the present and into the future. Although the Jewish patterns of keeping time revolve around the Exodus from Egypt, the Christian calendar is centered on the life and ministry of Jesus.

The church year begins four Sundays before Christmas with Advent. This season—often commemorated with the lighting of an Advent wreath—is a time of expectation and hope. Advent not only looks back to the first coming of Jesus but also anxiously waits for and calls upon Christ to come back quickly. "Come, Lord Jesus Christ. Come and make all things new!" Advent forms a people who can be patient with God's gracious redemption of all things.

If you took a survey of Christian college students and asked them what biblical verse is their favorite, I am convinced that Jeremiah 29:11 would win. "I know the plans I have in mind for you, declares the LORD; they are plans for peace, not disaster, to give you a future filled with hope" (CEB). I suspect that college-age students love that verse because they are sure it means God has a job for them when they graduate.

However, few people ever pay attention to Jeremiah 29:10: "The LORD proclaims: When Babylon's *seventy years* are up, I will come and fulfill my gracious promise to bring you back to this place. I know the plans I have in mind for you . . ." (with v. 11*a*, CEB, emphasis added). Verse 10 invites the people to live patiently through seventy years of exile knowing that God will fulfill his promise for a hope and future. I tell those same college students that God promises to find them a job by the time they reach the age of ninety-two.

In a world where the pace of life continually speeds up, where everything has to come fast, and where attention spans are rapidly declining, it might be wonderfully transformative and counterformative for a people to every year spend four weeks shaped by the patient endurance of God. Advent invites the people of God to endure. It invites them to pray expectantly. It forms people who know that justice and righteousness will not come fully through any human institution or plan but will only break out completely when Christ comes to renew all things.

The season of Advent is followed by Christmas and the weeks of Epiphany. In those days together the church celebrates the coming of the light of Christ into the darkness. In Epiphany the church not only celebrates the coming of the light but is also formed to be a reflection of that divine light to the surrounding world.

Perhaps the most transformative period of the year for the church is the Lenten season. During those forty days of fasting and confession, disciples of Jesus walk together beneath the shadow of the cross not only to remember and confess their human tendencies toward sin and violence but also to be reminded of a grace that is greater than their sin.

Lent ends with Holy Week and the practices connected with Palm Sunday, Maundy Thursday, and Good Friday. Palm Sunday, on the one hand, is that ironic day when the church shouts "Hosanna" and celebrates that Jesus is the world's one true Lord and the fulfillment of Israel's hopes for a messiah. But on the other hand, Palm Sunday serves as a reminder that as Christians we still have so much to discover about the upside-down nature of this kingdom led by a Ruler who rides on a donkey, leads by serving, and conquers by dying. One of my favorite Lenten traditions is keeping the palm branches used in the Palm Sunday service for a year, letting them dry out, grinding them, burning them, and using the ash for next year's Ash Wednesday.

During Holy Week followers of Jesus gather around the Lord's Table on Maundy Thursday (*maundy* is derived from a Latin word meaning "command," referring to Jesus's new commandment of John 13:34) and are reminded that the Lord of all creation is a servant who washes the feet of his followers. Jesus is the King who invites his people to be first by being last and to lead by being a servant.

There are several traditions that surround Good Friday. Perhaps my favorite tradition is the Tenebrae service (from another Latin term meaning "shadows"). Tenebrae services often include the telling of the gospel story accompanied by the lighting of candles. Then in the middle of the service the focus turns toward the story of the crucifixion. The candles are then extinguished one by one as the body of Christ is reminded again of the betrayal, denial, and fleeing of the disciples. The service ends with the extinguishing of the Christ candle. Good Friday services often end in darkness and silence so that the people can return on Sunday and experience the beauty, power, and light of the resurrected Christ.

In the church calendar Easter is not just a day but also a season in which the church dwells within the current reality and the future hope of the resurrection. The seven weeks of Easter culminate with Pentecost Sunday and the celebration of the coming of the Holy Spirit and the birth of the church. Many Christian traditions extend the primary weeks of the church year one additional Sunday with a focus on the Trinity. On that day the people of God reflect on the beauty of God's self-revelation in the creative work of the Father, the redemptive work of the Son, and the continued sanctifying work of the Holy Spirit.

The rest of the church year is called Common Time or Ordinary Time. During this season it is often the tradition to focus on the continuing mission of God through the church in the everyday, ordinary life of his people.

The ongoing life of the church has also been marked across the centuries by participation in what are called sacraments. In particular, the people of God have thought about baptism and the Lord's Supper (or Eucharist) as unique means or methods the Spirit of God uses to form the church. For this reason they are also often referred to as *means of grace*. They are viewed as practices distinctively filled with transformational meaning and grace.

The practice of baptism is rooted in the Exodus story. At the banks of the Red Sea the people were caught between the waters of chaos (remember the *tohu* and *bohu*) and Pharaoh's attempt to recapture and re-enslave them. Moses lifted up his staff, and the people entered the water as slaves, but they came out of the water as God's new people. In the early pages of each of the Gospels, John the Baptist invites people to come out to the wilderness (the place where God formed Israel) and once again pass through the waters and be prepared for the new kingdom coming into the world. In the Epistles, Paul connects baptism to the death and resurrection of Jesus. To be baptized for Paul is to enter the water in identification with the death of Jesus so that one can by faith come out of the water as a participant in the new creation initiated in the resurrection of Christ.

Baptism not only connects a person by faith to the death and resurrection of Jesus but also initiates that person into the community of the church. Often in the early church the genders were baptized separately so that people could leave their old clothes behind as they entered the water. When they came out, the church was waiting for them with white robes symbolizing not only their new life in Christ but also their inclusion with the "saints robed in white" (see Rev. 7:14).

I was once preparing a group of college-age new believers for baptism. I was passionately talking with them about the significance of putting to death the old life and entering into the new creation. I was also trying to help them celebrate not only the connection they would now have with the church of Jesus Christ across history but also the significant link the parts of Christ's body have with one another. One of the young women, quite exasperated, said, "I'm not sure I am ready for this!"

I thought she was perhaps nervous about sharing her testimony (which was a tradition at that church as part of the baptism liturgy). I said, "You'll do great. Don't be nervous. Just share what Jesus has done in your life and you'll do fine."

She responded, "Oh, I don't care about that! What just dawned on me is that after this is over, everything will be different. You and I will be brother and sister. And I'm not sure I'm ready for that."

Thankfully she eventually decided she was ready. Twenty years later, she still reminds me regularly that even though we now live in different states, we are still brother and sister in the Lord and that she is not letting me out of my baptismal obligations any time soon.

Another key sacramental practice of the church is partaking in the Lord's Supper. This eucharistic or thanksgiving meal not only tells again the story of the sacrificial love of God revealed in Jesus Christ but also serves as a means of grace to form the church into the body of Christ. There is an old diet line that says, "You are what you eat." Nowhere is that more the case than when disciples of Jesus are gathered around the Lord's Table. The Table is the gospel enacted. In a broken and sinful world, the church gathers around the Lord's broken body and shed blood in order to become the firstfruits of the new creation.

There are so many other practices that could be mentioned. There are practices that have historically been important as part of worship: a call to worship, songs of praise, passing of the peace, giving of tithes and offerings, prayers of confession and assurance, prayers and anointing for the sick, the reading of the Scriptures, preaching, the recitation of creeds, and the receiving of a blessing and benediction (to name just a few).

And there are significant practices in the mission of the church: acts of compassion, evangelism, witness, mercy, forgiveness, reconciliation, and calls for justice. Some of these I will expand on in the final chapter.

We could also spend time thinking about personal spiritual disciplines such as study, prayer, fasting, silence, service, confession, journaling, and even rest.

The point of this chapter has not been to name and describe all of the corporate and individual practices that are available for the growth and development of the life of the church. There are many wonderful resources across the history of Christianity to draw from to better know how to be immersed into various means of grace. The point here has been to simply say that a people who embrace exile have to participate in practices that form and habituate the life of the church and those within it to the life of faithfulness to the kingdom.

A people in exile need a story to sustain them. But unless that same people participate repeatedly in rehabituating practices, they will simply keep quacking their amens and then waddling home.

Questions for Discussion

- How does the duck parable speak to you? Are there areas of kingdom faithfulness to which you think the church often quacks its amens but that it fails to embody in the world?

- Does the concept of "cultural liturgies" make sense to you? What are some examples of ways through repetition you think the world squeezes people into its mold?

- What does it mean to think of the church's practices as counterformative? How effective do you think the church today is at counterformation?

- What have been some of the most important practices in the life of the church for your spiritual formation?

5

BLESSING BABYLON

A job is a vocation only if someone else calls you to do it for them rather than for yourself. And so our work can be a calling only if it is reimagined as a mission of service to something beyond merely our own interests. Thinking of work mainly as a means of self-fulfillment and self-realization slowly crushes a person.

—Timothy Keller, *Every Good Endeavor*

● ● ●

At most you will spend about 5 percent of your waking hours in [church]. Ninety-five percent of your life you spend in the world. . . . The scorecard is about the 95 percent [lived] out in the world.

—Pastor Victor Pentz, quoted in Amy Sherman, *Kingdom Calling*

● ● ●

The LORD of heavenly forces, the God of Israel, proclaims to all the exiles I have carried off from Jerusalem to Babylon: Build houses and settle down; cultivate gardens and eat what they produce. Get married and have children; then help your sons find wives and your daughters find husbands in order that they too may have children. Increase in number there so that you don't dwindle away. Promote the welfare of the city where I have sent you into exile. Pray to the LORD for it, because your future depends on its welfare.

—Jer. 29:4-7, CEB

● ● ●

I was recently invited to speak at a conference for pastors and leaders where the theme was exile. Borrowing from *The Wizard of Oz*, the theme for the week was titled "Toto, We're Not in Kansas Anymore!" (ironically, the conference was in Kansas). There were many clever insights made during the week by speakers comparing Dorothy's sojourn in Oz and the church's sense of twenty-first-century displacement. However, there was one place where I thought the use of Oz as a metaphor kept breaking down—the yellow brick road. For Dorothy and her friends, the yellow brick road is the path to follow into and hopefully out of Oz. The answer to Dorothy's desire to get back home is, "Follow the yellow brick road."

The shocking thing about the word of the prophets to those in exile is that they don't really encourage the people to look for, pray for, or try to discover a way out. Rather, the people are invited to settle down and work.

I included at the beginning of this chapter a powerful text from the prophet Jeremiah. The Lord's command through the prophet is not to try and escape exile. The word is not to live isolated and hidden lives until exile is over. Rather, the word is to "promote the welfare of the city where I have sent you into exile" (Jer. 29:7, CEB). The Lord encourages the people to work, to have children, and to promote the well-being of Babylon. The people aren't to go find a yellow brick road out. They are to settle in and find ways to work where they are.

Another shocking prophetic word in exile comes from Isaiah. Isaiah 40 serves as the first word to the people of Judah now that they are in exile. The people lament in Babylon that they have been abandoned by God and by all the nations that used to value them. Lamentations 1 keeps repeating this phrase about the nation of Judah: "She has no one to comfort her. . . . There is no one to comfort her" (vv. 2, 17, NRSV). But then the voice of Isaiah breaks through the grief, "Comfort, O comfort my people, says your God" (Isa. 40:1, NRSV). The prophet proclaims that God has not forgotten his people. Instead God plans to comfort and save them.

A divinely inspired voice cries out to the exiles:

In the wilderness prepare the way of the LORD,
    make straight in the desert a highway for our God.
Every valley shall be lifted up,
    and every mountain and hill be made low;
the uneven ground shall become level,
    and the rough places a plain.
Then the glory of the LORD shall be revealed,
    and all people shall see it together,
    for the mouth of the LORD has spoken. (Vv. 3-5, NRSV).

What a beautiful word! God has not forgotten his people in exile. He sees them. He knows them. He comforts them.

He also has instructions for them. Notice first of all that the instructions come "in the wilderness" or "in the desert." They are not instructions for how to get out of the location of exile. Instead they are a word spoken in the place of dislocation.

The primary instructions are to get out and work on the highway. Like a good road crew, the people are supposed to go out and find crooked places and make them straight. Find rough places to smooth and potholes to fill. If you are thinking along with me, perhaps this is the place where the metaphor of the yellow brick road leading out of exile might actually work. But notice the purpose of the roadwork for Isaiah. The goal is not to fix the highway so the people can get out. The objective of all the roadwork is so that the glory of the Lord can come in and all people—including, I assume, the Babylonian people who took Judah into exile—can see God's glory together.

So what are God's instructions to exiles? Build houses in Babylon. Get married and have children. Seek the welfare of those around them. In other words, go to work.

Work Is Good

Having the opportunity and ability to work is a really good thing. We were made to work and create. If we return to the great hymn of creation from Genesis 1, we find that when God created human beings in his image, he gave to them a series of commands: "Be fertile and multiply, and fill the earth and subdue it" (v. 28, NRSV). There appears to be three parts to this divine mandate. First, the command given to Adam and Eve is to "be fertile" or "be fruitful and multiply." This is a wonderful cocreational mandate that lets humankind know that God never gets tired of being in relationship with people. When people have children, God doesn't think, *Oh no! Not another one!* Rather, just as most parents celebrate the birth of a new child as the greatest day in their lives, so also does God rejoice at the opportunity to love another of his most valued creatures.

The third part of the command—to "subdue" or have dominion over creation—is not a directive giving permission for humans to exploit the earth (or the earth's creatures) in whatever way they see fit. Rather, God wants people to be co-gardeners with him as they care for creation. The obligation placed upon humans as God's image or reflection is to have dominion over—to give loving care to—all things, imitating God's heart and participating in God's gracious oversight of all he created.

But it's the second part of the command that I especially want to focus on here. It is the divine decree to "fill the earth" that theologians often find fascinating. In particular, the great Dutch theologian and statesman Abraham Kuyper saw in this second part of the command a "cultural mandate" to use the giftedness given to human persons to creatively fill the world with what people make and form to the glory of God.[1]

I had a professor who used to lecture on God's "cultural mandate," and he would try to illustrate it using this story. "Imagine," he would say, "that one day Eve comes to Adam and says, 'Adam, I'm going for a walk. Would you please clean up your corner of the garden? Quit leaving your dirty fig leaves lying all around. Pick up before I get back.' So Adam gets down on his hands and knees and tries to clean up. But then Adam realizes the more he tries to pick up, the dirtier he gets. So he picks up a branch off the ground and starts using it to move leaves around instead. It works okay, but then he puts a couple other branches with it and ties them together and discovers he can clean even more effectively with a group of branches bound together. Eve returns and asks, 'Adam, what are you doing?' Adam looks at her with bewilderment in his eyes and says, 'I think I'm using this broom to sweep up the garden.'"

My professor would say that already there are at least three other entities in the garden besides Adam, Eve, and God. Now there is a tool: a broom. There is a job: sweeping. And pretty soon there will be an occupation (Adam will now be in charge of sweeping on odd days, and Eve on the even days). The point of the illustration is that it doesn't take long for humans to fill the garden with that which their God-given ingenuity and creativity has produced. My professor would conclude the lecture by saying, "Adam and Eve probably created so much stuff that when they were kicked out of the garden, they were forced to rent a U-Haul."

The point is simply this: theologically, the people of God are convinced that it is a good thing for people to work. We are created to use the giftedness given to us by God to contribute to the goodness, the beauty, and the well-being of the world.

Sacred and Secular

One of my seminary friends was given a custodial job at a local church while we were both students. His primary assignment was to vacuum all of the carpeted areas and polish and clean all of the tiled places in the building. He had business cards printed up that said, "Pastor Joe—Minister to the Floors." His friends were a little bit amused at how proud Joe was of his self-appointed title. But twenty-five years later, I still remember how seriously and diligently Joe took his responsibilities as the minister to the floors. For the last several years Joe has been serving as a staff member at a very large church in the Southeast. His responsibilities have extended far beyond taking care of the floors in the church. However, I can't help but think that the care and energy he put into what may have been treated by most as a menial role set patterns of diligence and faithfulness that have served him—and the kingdom of God—well no matter what role he has been given.

A problem that developed on the significance of work among God's people was the division between sacred and secular work. Of the twelve tribes that descended from Jacob (or Israel), one tribe—the Levites—were chosen by God to devote their life to the care of the temple and nurture of all of the spiritual practices associated with it. Because they were a priestly tribe, the Levites were not given land and so they were supported through the tithes of the other eleven tribes as they gave back to God through the temple.

It is easy to see how people could begin to associate the work of the Levites as the sacred or "spiritual" work and begin to view all of the other tasks for sustaining the life of the community—farming, herding, protecting, building, ruling, judging, parenting, and so on—as less than holy, or as secular. The word *secular* comes from a Latin term that means "of this time" or "of this age." I think it is very unfortunate when Christian people begin to believe that the work of priests or ministers is sacred and connected to God and that the work of the laity—especially the work done outside the walls of the church—is secular, or just part of the realities of the present age.

One of the theological correctives that may need to take place for many in the body of Christ is for the line between the sacred and the secular to be blurred, if not eliminated. Another great quote from Abraham Kuyper comes from his inaugural address at the dedication of the Free University of Amsterdam. In that address lauding the need for people of faith to be prepared for every field of endeavor, Kuyper proclaimed, "There is not a square inch in the whole domain of our human existence over which Christ, who is Sovereign over all, does not cry: 'Mine!'"[2] If Kuyper is correct (and I believe he is), then there is no place, no responsibility, and no work that can't be at some level sacred, holy, or caught up in God's purposes.

I find that the divide between sacred and secular often occurs in our imaginations as it is applied to business. There is a line that is spoken in almost every mafia movie right before the godfather or crime boss has an associate killed. He looks with melancholy at his victim and says, "It's not personal. It's business." Somehow that's supposed to morally justify the act.

My sense is that Christians use a similar line of thinking about their day-to-day work. Some people are convinced "It's not spiritual. It's business." But again, if Kuyper is correct, it is all spiritual.

The word *economy* is taken from a Greek word that means "household" (the word is *oikonomia*). The idea of the economy is that the work to which people commit themselves is part of a larger household of connections where the members of that society or economy serve one another, care for one another, and even minister to one another through their work. Like a caring household where every person has important tasks and responsibilities to fulfill in order for the home to function efficiently, the work we do fulfills a particular role in the *oikonomia*, in the household of a community.

That means that Nick, who many mornings serves me a skinny vanilla latte at my neighborhood Starbucks, is part of the community household where he is the minister of coffee. Carlos, who for so many years made sure our cars ran safely and consistently, is a minister of transportation. Beth, who taught our kids algebra, is our favorite minister of math. Megan, who cuts what hair I have remaining, is my minister of style. Scott is our minister of insurance, making sure that if something goes horribly wrong, we will be okay. Tim was our minister of finding the right house to live in and then of finding someone to buy it when it was time to move away. Gus and his crew are the ministers to many of the lawns in the neighborhood. The list could go on and on. But that doesn't even scratch the surface of the many intersections and connections each of those people make possible. Take my favorite barista, Nick, for example. The cups of coffee he serves each morning are connected to bean growers, harvesters, roasters, packagers, transporters, designers, marketers, builders, accountants, cup manufacturers, foresters, paper millers, dairy farmers, milk processors, carton designers, oil refiners, plastic fabricators, vanilla-flavor producers, sugarcane growers, coffee-machine creators, and on and on—all present and connected to one skinny vanilla latte. Not only do those connections make that cup of coffee possible, but their interconnections also make the lives and well-being of the people connected possible. There is something about work done well for the sake of the *oikonomia* that is beautiful and holy. It is not simply secular; it has the hints of God's mercy and care—hints of his holiness—reflected within it.

Eschatology

Another theological area that has probably damaged our understanding of the significance of work is our eschatology. The word *eschatology* means the "study of last things." A person's eschatology is how he or she thinks God's story of creation is going to end.

During the seventeenth, eighteenth, and early nineteenth centuries in the West, the eschatological hopes for most Christians were quite optimistic. For many people during that time most aspects of life, health, and well-being were improving. There was a sense that the world was advancing. And for many Christians there was even a sense that God's kingdom was increasing and growing—that things on earth were beginning to reflect significant aspects of heaven.

But after the Civil War in the middle of the nineteenth century, there were some Christians whose hopes began to shift. The eschatological hopes for earth began to become very small, and all of the hope was placed far off in heaven. After the horrors of the two world wars at the start of the twentieth century, the eschatological hopes among Western Christians became very otherworldly. Most generations of Christians living today have not been shaped to believe that God might redeem the entire creation. Rather, most have been shaped to believe that the end of the gospel story is the escape of the people of God from the world, the destruction of the earth, and the entrance of all the faithful into a completely different location separate from the temporality and materiality of the world.

I think this kind of eschatology has deeply scarred our understanding of work. Not only have many of us divided the sacred from the secular, but we also have come to see the work of our hands as temporary, transitory, and thus somewhat meaningless.

At its worst this view has exacerbated humankind's exploitation of creation. Why should we concern ourselves with the caretaking of the earth when it is simply a temporary stop on the way to eternity? It is as though the earth is simply a place humans are renting for a while and therefore they don't have to be overly concerned with its well-being.

In the latter part of the twentieth century and on into the first part of the twenty-first, some theologians began to question the veracity of such an escapist eschatology. The hopes for most early Christians—and in particular the apostle Paul—were connected to the resurrection of the body and the renewal of creation (see especially Rom. 8 or 1 Cor. 15). For Paul, the whole creation is groaning along with the followers of Jesus awaiting the redemption of the whole world. The idea that our bodies would be resurrected—in the same manner that Christ was resurrected—means that our materiality (our connection to the earth) may not be a temporary state but may be part and parcel of what it means to be human. Our eschatological hope as Christians is not an escape from the body but the renewal and redemption of life in the body. Our eschatological hope is not that the heavens and the earth would be destroyed but that God's will would "be done on earth as it is in heaven" (Matt. 6:10, NRSV).

Many theologians and scholars argue that hoping that God's redemption and salvation would include all of creation is not a new theology but a return to a hopeful eschatology that somehow went astray for a century or two.

If this is indeed the case that we are not just waiting to be rescued from earth but are called to partake in the care and the redemption of creation, then work is not just something believers do to pay bills until Christ returns. Rather, work is part of our participation in God's redemptive care and work for the whole world. N. T. Wright says it very well:

Jesus's resurrection is the beginning of God's new project not to snatch people away from earth to heaven but to colonize earth with the life of heaven. That, after all, is what the Lord's Prayer is about.[3]

. . . The point of the resurrection . . . is that *the present bodily life is not valueless just because it will die*. . . . What you do with your body in the present matters because God has a great future in store for it. . . . What you *do* in the present—by painting, preaching, singing, sewing, praying, teaching, building hospitals, digging wells, campaigning for justice, writing poems, caring for the needy, loving your neighbor as yourself—*will last into God's future*. These activities are not simply ways of making the present life a little less beastly, a little more bearable, until the day when we leave it behind altogether. . . . They are part of what we may call *building for God's kingdom*.[4]

A Warning

No theology of work would be complete without a warning about the ways that work can be captured and distorted by sin. The creation story not only celebrates the work of filling and tending the garden that was given to humankind but also narrates the ways Adam and Eve used the gifts of dominion and creativity to transcend the boundaries set down by God and so begin to misuse creation and one another.

It is clearly easy for human work and endeavor to become ways of exploiting other people. Money and resources in and of themselves are not evil, but from the beginning they have easily led to greed, manipulation, exploitation, injustice, and violence.

Humans are uniquely created to be images or reflections of God to one another and to creation. And so as we work and care for others inside and outside the home, and inside or outside the walls of the church, the question is, Are we working in ways that reflect the love, the mercy, the justice, the goodness, and the hospitality of God? Or are we working in ways that are failing to reflect his redemptive hopes and his saving purposes?

The goal of God's people in Babylon is not to plan their escape. The goal is to live and work as salt and light in order to bless Babylon and to allow people to see the good work that they do as a reflection of the glory and goodness of God.

Questions for Discussion

- How do you think the work that you have been given blesses the *oikonomia*, or the household of the community?

- What problems do you think have been created by dividing the sacred and the secular or by having an escapist view of eschatology?

- What do you think are the primary traps of sin related to work?

RAISING RESIDENT ALIENS

The greatest issue facing the world today, with all its heartbreaking needs, is whether those who, by profession or culture, are identified as "Christians" will become disciples—students, apprentices, practitioners—of Jesus Christ, steadily learning from him how to live the life of the Kingdom of the Heavens into every corner of human existence.

—Dallas Willard, *The Great Omission*

● ● ●

If teenagers lack an articulate faith, maybe it is because the faith we show them is too spineless to merit much in the way of conversation. Maybe teenagers' inability to talk about religion is not because the church inspires a faith too deep for words, but because the God-story that we tell is too vapid to merit more than a superficial vocabulary.

—Kenda Creasy Dean, *Almost Christian*

● ● ●

In the future, when your children ask you, "What do these stones mean?" tell them that the flow of the Jordan was cut off before the ark of the covenant of the LORD.

—Josh. 4:6-7, NIV

● ● ●

There are over 200,000 Armenians living in and around Glendale in Southern California. Many Armenians escaped to the United States and elsewhere during the Armenian Genocide (also known as the Armenian Holocaust), when the Ottoman Empire and its successor state, the Republic of Turkey, attempted to systematically exterminate 1.5 million Armenians between 1915 and 1917. Because Glendale is close to Pasadena, we had several Armenian families in the church I pastored there. They are wonderful and beautiful people for many reasons. But my favorite thing about our Armenian friends was their food. It didn't take long for my family and me to start spreading hummus on everything!

I loved being invited into the homes of our Armenian friends not just for amazing dinners but also for the unbelievable stories of escape from persecution, life in an unfamiliar place, hard work to survive and thrive, and gratitude for God's faithfulness.

I'll never forget one meal with some of my favorite people in the world—the Maljian family. It was a big meal. All six in our family were there, and Minas and Sonia Maljian made sure their two sons—Peter and Rafi—were there with their wives and children. There were lots of mouths to feed, but there were still leftovers at the end.

During dinner Minas and Sonia told stories about their memories of immigration and their hard work as a tailor and a nurse that had made their lives and the lives of their boys possible. But I found myself most interested when Sonia—in a good-hearted way—began to lament some of the lost Armenian identity in her sons' generation. Although she loves both of her amazing daughters-in-law, we laughed about the fact that neither of them are Armenian. There is actually a term for it in the Armenian community; it's called marrying an *odar* (literally, a "foreigner"). Of all the particular cultural groups in that area of California, a higher percentage of Armenians marry within their ethnic community than any other minority group in the population. Each year, however, the percentage declines.

Sonia bemoaned that even though she and Minas had taken their sons to Armenian language school every Saturday when they were boys, now as adults they rarely spoke the language, could not write it very well, and were not teaching it to their children.

Although Sonia was clearly concerned about the loss of her sons' ethnic particularity and language, she was making sure that her children and grandchildren knew how to cook Armenian and that they knew the stories of where the family had come from and what their ancestors had endured.

My dear friends the Maljians seemed to intuitively understand how hard it is for the children of a particular ethnic identity to maintain their uniqueness without being absorbed and assimilated into the all-encompassing and homogenizing American culture. Raising resident aliens is a tenuous task. On the one hand, Minas and Sonia desperately wanted their children to thrive and flourish within the competitive and market-driven American society. But on the other hand, a big part of them did not want their Armenian identity to be at best trivialized and at worst lost in succeeding generations. They had endured too much sustaining their ethnicity in the face of persecution in Turkey to have it erased by ease in America. They knew it would not take long for Peter and Rafi to stop living as Armenians navigating their way through a hospitable but still foreign nation and become Americans who eat hummus from a tub purchased at the grocery store (*real* hummus is homemade).

The Maljian family was struggling with a truth I came to several years ago while working on my degree in ethics. Much of the reading I was doing in my studies led me to believe that our actions as human beings flow from three core areas: our values, our identity, and our convictions. At the time I was thinking about how ineffective preaching is at bringing about transformation when it focuses on people's actions without addressing the deeper realities of a person's values, identity, and convictions. The same could be said for parenting (and perhaps even more so). As parents we often focus on the actions (good and bad) that our kids are doing without thinking about or addressing our children's values, their identity, and the convictions from which their actions flow.

To say it another way, the Maljians seemed to understand that if they wanted their boys to continue to act like Armenians, they needed to keep treasuring Armenian ideals, keep understanding and identifying themselves as Armenians, and have convictions that helped them interpret the world as Armenians. This is, by the way, why Sonia in particular was right. She knew that if she was going to raise Peter and Rafi to be resident aliens, the eating matters, language matters, and imagination matters.

The biblical book that also understands these issues and is most interested in raising resident aliens is the book of Daniel. The powerful Major Prophet seems to know how easy it is for the young to be assimilated quickly into the surrounding culture. The book of Daniel recognizes that if the Judeans weren't careful, at some point their children would cease to be Judeans living in exile in Babylon and would instead become Babylonians who attended the synagogue on occasion.

It shouldn't be a surprise that a book obsessed with raising resident aliens in exile also understands that eating matters, language matters, and imagination matters.

You Are What You Eat

The book of Daniel opens with a story about eating. King Nebuchadnezzar invited Daniel and his three Judean friends—Hananiah, Mishael, and Azariah—to prepare for leadership in the Babylonian Empire and to eat from the allotments served daily at the king's own table. However, "Daniel resolved not to defile himself with the royal food and wine, and he asked the chief official for permission not to defile himself this way" (Dan. 1:8, NIV). What ensues is a kind of test of God's faithfulness. Daniel and his friends forgo the meat of Nebuchadnezzar and instead grow stronger on a diet of vegetables than do those who keep eating with the king.

I do not think that the story is meant to elevate the nutritional value of vegetables over meat (although that may indeed be the case). If this text is simply about one diet being superior to another, it ceases to be about God's miraculous faithfulness to obedient exiles. Rather, I am convinced that the story has to do with the challenge Babylon poses to the desires of the Judeans. Daniel and his friends seem to know that if they allow their appetites and desires to be defined by the king and his table, they will be fully captured by Babylon.

The culture around us—like the culture of Babylon—traffics in desire. Our loves or our desires are not totally innate. Desires and values are nurtured and trained. Our hearts learn to want the right or the wrong things. What Daniel fears is that the meat of the king will lead to the corruption of his desires. If he learns to love what the Babylonian king has to offer, he has enslaved himself to the empire. For ultimately, you are what you love.

If the church in the current age is going to raise resident aliens, the people of God have to have hard conversations about the values that are modeled and taught to our children. The primary commodities of life are time, money, and energy. When our children observe our lives, where do they see us investing those commodities? What priority do we give to spiritual growth? When the limits of time force us to say no to things, what area gets compromised? Where is our treasure placed? Are our children aware of where the family's resources are invested? Are our children ever called to sacrifice as part of their kingdom identity? Do they ever observe their parents living sacrificially out of a love for God's kingdom?

Values and desires are competitive with one another. Our hearts are not easily shared. "No one can serve two masters" (Matt. 6:24, NIV).

Identity and "We" Confusion

We not only act out of our values, but we also respond based on our identity. My two oldest sons are very good friends, but they are very different from one another. Both act out of their unique identities. Caleb is a really gifted student. He seemed to come out of the womb voraciously reading one book after another. He knows he is a good student. It's a huge part of his identity. I know that he walks into any class on the first day thinking, *I am going to get an A in this class. How long will it take before the teacher realizes how bright I am?*

Our son Noah is equally gifted, but academics have not yet been the source of his identity. Noah entered the world big and brash. He is a party waiting to happen. When Noah was in his stroller as an infant, he would wave his arms in an attempt to get people's attention so he could smile at them and see if they would smile or laugh in return. I know that he walks into any class on the first day thinking, I am the most likable person in this room. *How long will it take before the teacher (and everyone else in the room) realizes how funny I am?*

I'm not completely sure where those identities came from (I have a few theories), but I know my sons act out of them. We all act out of who we believe ourselves to be.

Identity is also very important in the book of Daniel. When the four main characters in the book arrive in Babylon, they have Judean names. In Hebrew Daniel's name means "God is my judge"; Hananiah's name means "the Lord is gracious"; Mishael's name means "who is like God?"; and Azariah's name means "the Lord has helped." Nebuchadnezzar, however, gives them new names connected to new identities. He names Daniel *Belteshazzar*, meaning "Bel protects the king." Hananiah is renamed *Shadrach*, meaning "the command of Aku." Mishael is given the name *Meshach*, meaning "the gods move with force." And Azariah is to be called *Abednego*, meaning "the servant of Nebo." Nebuchadnezzar clearly wants their primary identities to be less associated with Yahweh and his faithful connection to Judah's past and more connected with their new "home" and the gods of Babylon.

The most famous narrative in the book of Daniel—the casting of Shadrach, Meshach, and Abednego (notice we remember their Babylonian identities) into the furnace of fire for not bowing to Nebuchadnezzar's image—is a story about the struggle for identity. We often think of this great act of deliverance by God as a story about worship. We tend to think God rescues the Hebrew children because they refuse to worship Nebuchadnezzar. Yet in reality it is a story about citizenship as much as it is about worship. Nebuchadnezzar is not bothered that these three Hebrew kids worship Yahweh. He'll take as many gods as he can stack up on Babylon's side. The problem is a question of loyalty. In a ceremony of allegiance not too far removed from the opening exercises that take place every morning in every elementary school (Christian or public) in America (and I assume in most other countries also), Nebuchadnezzar wants them to show that despite their commitment to Yahweh, their primary identity and thus their primary allegiance is connected to Babylon. In most of the world's great Babylons religion is only a problem when and if it gets in the way of citizenship and national allegiance.

I often refer to this identity problem as "we" confusion. When my wife and I first got married, she would often say things such as, "I think *we* really need to take out the trash," "*We* really need to get the car worked on," and "Don't you think it's time *we* mowed the lawn?" It took me a while to realize that when she said *we*, she really meant *me*. I often found myself saying things such as, "It's probably time *we* made dinner." Twenty-six years later, she's still waiting for that to happen.

A people trying to raise resident aliens have to work hard at helping their kids work through "we" confusion. Who is the primary "we" that forms our identity? Is our primary "we" the universal church—Christ's body connected to one another throughout the world? Or is our primary "we" the nation? Is our "we" a particular social class? God forbid, is our primary "we" a particular race?

Like the three thrown in the furnace, I take this "we" stuff pretty seriously. Driving around town I have noticed a number of church reader boards that say things such as, "Pray for *our* election" and "Pray for *our* troops." These kinds of sayings cause me to twinge a bit.

As I write this, America has just been through a presidential election. It was a pretty rugged and divisive campaign. I think it is very important that the church that I am part of prays for the election of the American president. No doubt the welfare of both America and the Christian church in America will be impacted by the recent election results. However, this election was not the election of "our" president. The church doesn't have a president. America has a president, but the church proclaims that the world has only one true Lord and Ruler over creation. Jesus Christ, the resurrected Son of God, is Lord of the church no matter who lives in the White House.

It is critical that the church prays for America's service men and women. Many in the church have served and are serving in the nation's armed forces. Many who are part of the church have lost their lives in the service of the country. But as important as it is for the church to honor and pray for all those in the world who risk their lives in the pursuit of peace, "we" don't have troops. Nations have military forces, but the church lives as a people who have laid down the sword and taken up the cross.

What I am proposing is not just a semantic game. Certainly every person lives daily out of several different identities—often at the same time. Today I have lived as a father, a son, a husband, a pastor, a professor, a writer, a neighbor, an Idahoan, a disappointed Seattle Mariner fan, and an election-obsessed American—just to name a few. The question is about what our primary identity is. I think the issue of primary identity is what Jesus had in mind when he spoke of going through a new birth. It is certainly what the apostle Paul had in mind when he pictured baptism as a participation in the death of Christ, only to rise from the water identifying with the new-creation life of the resurrection.

"We" confusion is tricky. The people of God must form their children as those who identify first and foremost with Christ and his people. If we do not, it is too easy to lose the uniqueness of living as Christians who happen to live in America and discover that we—and our children—have become Americans who attend church when time permits.

Language and Imagination

A lot of the book of Daniel has to do with language. Again in the opening narrative, the four Hebrew young men are not only invited to the table of Nebuchadnezzar and given new names but also taught the Aramaic language. The book of Daniel is the only book in the Bible that comes to us in two written languages. In the oldest manuscripts available to the church, chapter 1 and chapters 8–12 are written in Hebrew, while chapters 2–7 are written in Aramaic. This has led some scholars to assume that Daniel is a book made up of two original sources cut and pasted together. That may be the case. But it may also be the case that the manuscripts were left in two languages because the very language of the book itself points to the challenge of living in two linguistic worlds—the Hebrew language of faith and the Aramaic language of the empire—at the same time.

Language is incredibly important. As many linguistic philosophers of the last century have pointed out, we don't see the world as it is; we see the world as it is interpreted through our language. It is as though whichever language becomes the heart language of the people will also become the kingdom or empire of their imaginations. Will Daniel and his friends dream and interpret the world in Hebrew or in Aramaic?

Language, together with its role in imagination, is also important in the final chapters of the book of Daniel. The strange apocalyptic language, found particularly in chapters 7–12, is not so much an attempt to peer into the future as it is a kind of language that unmasks the temporal nature of Babylon and the other empires that purport to be eternal. Apocalyptic language is like a pair of glasses that allows the Judeans in exile to imagine Babylon, not as an eternal, benevolent, and life-giving force, but as a temporary and hideous beast headed for destruction and over which the Son of Man has and will have final authority.

Thus how we worship and how we speak with our children matters.

Several years ago I was waiting with my son Caleb in a roller-coaster line at the Six Flags amusement park in Texas. It was a long line, and we were getting bored. The Six Flags Entertainment Corporation is based in Texas and is named for the six national flags that have historically flown over Texas. The six historic national flags fly just outside the park gates, and we could see them from where we were standing in line. I knew that Caleb had just taken Texas state history in school, and so I asked him to name the flags and tell me their stories of rising and falling over Texas. He did a good job recounting the various shifts in authority of the "empires" that have laid claim at one time or another to Texas. Being the mischievous person I am, I asked Caleb, "Son, what flag do you think will be the seventh flag that will fly over Texas?"

The woman standing in front of us who had been pretending not to be eavesdropping on our conversation whipped around and, looking at me with eyes afire, said, "Young man, there won't ever be a seventh flag over Texas!"

Caleb, waiting until she turned back around, leaned over and whispered in my ear, "Idolater!"

At first I was worried that I may have warped my child. But in later conversations with him I realized that the language we use as a family and the language we use as a church in worship were giving to Caleb a pair of interpretive lenses through which he could love and be proud of the country of his birth without turning it into the eternal kingdom. Whatever we were doing at the time, we've tried to keep at it, because he was clearly learning to speak like a resident alien.

It is hard to raise resident aliens. Just ask Minas and Sonia what it's like to raise distinctly Armenian sons in the cultural melting pot of Los Angeles. Just ask Daniel, Hananiah, Mishael, and Azariah what it's like to be young Hebrew men living in and being wooed by the constantly alluring Babylon.

Raising resident aliens is not any easier today. Thankfully in the Christian tradition in moments of infant baptism and dedication new parents get a chance to stand before the body of Christ and invite the community of faith to covenant to live, to pray, to eat, to play, to dream, to speak, to worship, to correct, and to help them raise another generation of faithful people whose desire is for the kingdom to come, whose identity is first and foremost connected to Christ, and whose imagination and convictions are built upon the Solid Rock.

Questions for Discussion

- How is trying to raise kids in the Christian faith like trying to raise cultural resident aliens?

- What do you think we learn from the stories in the book of Daniel about the challenges of raising young people to be uniquely Christian?

- What would raising our kids to follow Christ mean if we not only paid attention to their actions but also tried to shape their values, their identity, and their convictions (or imaginations)?

MORE THAN SURVIVORS

*After Constantine, blessedly bereft of powers of imposition,
the church must indeed be the message it wishes a
watchful world to hear and embrace.*

—Rodney Clapp, *A Peculiar People*

●●●

*Those in whom the Spirit comes to live are God's
new Temple. They are, individually and corporately,
places where heaven and earth meet.*

—N. T. Wright, *Simply Christian*

●●●

*He says,
"It is too light a thing that you should be my servant
    to raise up the tribes of Jacob
    and to restore the survivors of Israel;
I will give you as a light to the nations,
    that my salvation may reach to the end of the earth."*

—Isa. 49:6, NRSV

●●●

On May 3, 1999, three days before our son Jonah was born, we lived through a massive F5 tornado that killed eight people and caused vast destruction in Oklahoma City, where we were living at the time. My wife's aunt lived near us and had a storm cellar. I'll never forget all of us—our two little boys, my parents, Debbie's aunt and her dear friend, a 120-pound Labrador retriever, a hamster in a plastic ball, and an extremely pregnant wife—hunkered down together in a small dusty cellar praying for God's safety and for his protection. I will admit to being afraid.

I fear that the call to embrace exile may cause some to view the role of the church in this time and this place to be much like my family hunkered down in that cellar. If you captured my sincerity and deep concern in the last chapter—how difficult it is to form children in Babylon—it would be easy to become focused inward, hoping to sustain and maintain as many young people as possible until the storm passes.

The book of Isaiah—from chapter 40 onward—offers amazing words of comfort and hope to a people who feel they have lost almost everything and have no significant future. But perhaps the most remarkable word of hope is this one from chapter 49:

> He says,
> "It is too light a thing that you should be my servant
> to raise up the tribes of Jacob
> and to restore the survivors of Israel;
> I will give you as a light to the nations,
> that my salvation may reach to the end of the earth."
> (V. 6, NRSV)

It is Isaiah's divinely inspired hope that not only would the people survive exile and their children be protected and return to

Jerusalem and to the Land of Promise, but also somehow while embracing exile, the people would become a light to the nations; that what happens to the people in exile would become the source of salvation not just for Judah but also for all people on the earth.

Embracing exile is not a pause in the missional purpose of God's people. Embracing exile may in fact be setting God's people free to rediscover their true mission and the powerful reasons for their divine creation in the first place.

I have become convinced that the book of Jonah is not just a book that retells the miraculous, and also frustrating, adventures of a prophet from the northern nation of Israel or Ephraim (see 2 Kings 14:25) but also a story formed and told by the southern nation of Judah as a way of reimagining or renarrating their own history.

In the same way that Jonah has a divine call upon his life, so, too, do the people of Judah stand before the Word of God and carry upon their lives a heavy call to live as reflections or images of God's love and mercy.

In the same way that Jonah ran from that call—going *down* to Tarshish (the mythical place of comfort) rather than getting *up* and going to Nineveh (the city of great evil)—so, too, were the Judeans disobedient to God's call to live as a holy nation uniquely reflecting the glory and goodness of Yahweh.

In the same way that the waters of chaos overwhelmed Jonah and the seafarers on the boat to Tarshish, so, too, did the *tohu* and the *bohu* of Babylon and Nebuchadnezzar come sweeping into Jerusalem.

In the same way that Jonah was swallowed up in a great fish and should have perished, so, too, were the Judeans swallowed up in exile, where their unique way of life and their glorious history should have met its end.

In the same way that Jonah discovered that God could meet him in the deepest and darkest pit of Sheol, so, too, did the Judeans learn that no longer having a holy city and a holy temple did not mean they had been deprived of God's holy presence.

And in the same way that Jonah was upchucked back into life and the divine call to be the source of redemption for Nineveh, so, too, did the disorientation of exile and the rubble of Jerusalem not invalidate the divine call and purpose the people of God still bore to be a light to the nations.

Like Jonah, embracing exile should not be the end of the church's purpose but may indeed be God's intentional action to renew and reestablish the purposes for which he formed his people in the first place. So let me close with some brief reflections on the opportunity this moment may be giving the church and what themes may help us to narrate this moment.

Releasing Colonialism and Revivalism

In those places where the church felt in charge—where the church sensed that it had "Christianized" the culture—much of its imagination for evangelization was shaped by forms of colonialism and revivalism.

Colonialism is the idea that the Christianization of a land (like Columbus's arrival in the New World) is synonymous with the adoption of the particular cultural customs and norms of the dominant and often invading culture. Much has been written in the last decades about the destructive nature of colonialism and the church's need to confess and repent of the violence and injustice often done in the name of Christ.

Abandoning a colonialist spirit seems obvious. But I think it is also necessary for the church that has embraced exile to give up many of the practices and perspectives of revivalism as well. As Rodney Clapp defines it,

> Revivalism aims to revive or revitalize the preexisting but now latent faith of birthright Christians. It presupposes a knowledge of the languages and practices of faith. . . .
>
> . . . It presumed not initiation into the transnational church but a reawakening of faith in the individual American—who, exactly as an American, was supposedly already something of a (Protestant) Christian.[1]

My own Christian tradition has been deeply shaped by the language and practices of American revivalism. This is not necessarily a bad thing. Like most Christians, there has been and still is much in my spiritual life that needs the Spirit's reviving from time to time. But what Clapp and others are saying is that for Christians living in an increasingly post-Christian culture, revivalism is a failed evangelism strategy because it assumes there is something latent in the hearts of people that simply needs to be rekindled. But it is hard to revive something that may in fact not be there at all.

In my most cynical moments, because revivalistic habits are hard to break, I have wondered in my own tradition if much of what we have recently thought of as church growth has in reality not been rooted in the redemption of lost people but has been mostly the reshuffling of discontented Christians from one church to another. No doubt there have been and continue to be people with remnant church memories whose connection to Christ and passion for faith are revived and revitalized, but unfortunately, for the most part the post-Christian world remains unchanged and unreached.

So what kinds of images, what kinds of visions, might a church that is embracing exile adopt as central to its mission? Let me briefly suggest four.

An Embodied Word

The gospel is always the good news of the reign of Jesus Christ proclaimed to the world. The church exists to proclaim the Word. Unfortunately we too often narrow the announcement of God's good news to what the church says or speaks audibly to the world.

In Pasadena there are a group of Christians who have taken upon themselves to regularly show up at big public events and shout through bullhorns at the crowd about the coming judgment of God. Each year at the Rose Parade, group members capitalize on the presence of a million or so people descending upon Colorado Boulevard and proclaim such good news to them as "God loves and kills!" or "The wages of sin is death!" A few years ago we were walking down the hill toward the Rose Bowl to attend a U2 concert when we ran into the bullhorn brigade shouting at the crowd. One of the megaphone preachers screamed, "Repent! You are all going to hell because all that you like is sex, drugs, and rock 'n' roll!" Rather than repenting, the crowd in unison shouted, "Woo-hoo!"

I am a preacher so I don't want to downplay the role of proclaiming or speaking the good news. Every week, the church gathers together to be reminded that the greatest news in the history of the world is that darkness does not get the last word, but light does.

Evil does not have the final word, but good wins out. Sin does not get the last word, but God's grace is sufficient. And death does not have the final say, because the resurrected Lord has conquered the grave. This is good news. This should be proclaimed with regularity and with boldness.

However, a people who have embraced exile know that the Word is not just proclaimed but also embodied. "The Word became flesh and lived among us" (John 1:14, NRSV). The good news must always be incarnate.

So the mission of the church in exile is not just to have a message but also to become the message. As Stanley Hauerwas says so often, "The church doesn't have a social strategy, the church *is* a social strategy"[2] or "The primary social task of the church is to be itself."[3]

An Open Table

If the proclamation of the gospel is not just about speaking good news but also about embodying the good news, then a people who embrace exile must recover a fuller, richer, and deeper ecclesiology than has most recently been the case.

There is much to be thankful for in the elevation of individual rights and freedoms that accompanied the Enlightenment. There is also much to celebrate in the Protestant and evangelical traditions' emphasis on having a personal relationship with Jesus Christ. But I often wonder if our rugged individualism and the emphasis on a personal faith have gone too far. The church should be more than a place people go; it should be something that by God's grace we are becoming.

This unity of the body is enacted regularly around the Lord's Table. There the faithful take in the broken body and shed blood of the Lord so that, by grace, they will become what they eat—the body of Christ broken for the sake of the world.

The Lord's Table is always open. There are always more seats available. The invitation is not to come to the table, grab what you need, and go ("eat it and beat it"). The invitation is to come and, through baptism and faith, join in the family of exiles.

One of my places of tension with the church growth movement has been around the issue of *homogenous units*. There is a theory within the church growth movement that people naturally want to be with people who are like themselves. That is the homogenous part. Like is attracted to like. So the theory encourages churches to figure out who they are and "market" themselves to people who fit those same categories. The problem I have with the theory is that it works. I have worked among college students for many years now. There is an old joke that is frequently told about college ministry: It isn't hard to grow a large college ministry. Just do two things. Always have free food and speak on three things: sex, the end times, and will there be sex in the end times. College kids will show up.

I'll admit to having some suspicion about monogenerational and monocultural congregations. It doesn't take the Spirit of God to get a group of white, middle-class conservatives together. It's called a country club. It doesn't take the Spirit to get a group of millennials together. It's called a concert.

What demands the Spirit and requires a broken body and shed blood is for people from different generations, different ethnicities, different cultures, different tastes, different political perspectives, and different social standings to gather around the Table of the

Lord and become one body. That requires the truly Pentecostal work of the Spirit. And that is the community of witness a divided and fractured world needs to behold and be invited to enter.

Clean Hearts

The church that embraces exile needs to be separated and filled so that it can be a blessing to the world. There will be an oddness about the people of God that is necessary for the sake of creation's redemption.

While we were living in Los Angeles, we would often go to shop and hang out at an unbelievable outdoor mall in Beverly Hills called the Grove. My children affectionately refer to it as the Temple of Consumption. Not only is it a beautiful place to shop on a warm California afternoon, but it is also the best place to see celebrities in the wild. Near the Grove are several synagogues, and many Orthodox Jewish families live in the surrounding neighborhoods. If our family made the trek from Pasadena to Beverly Hills, it was usually on a Friday evening or Saturday afternoon. Because the period between sundown on Friday and sundown on Saturday is the time of Sabbath observance for the Orthodox Jewish communities, we would often see large groups of worshippers walking (they won't drive on the Sabbath) to synagogue dressed in black. The men would all be wearing large hats and have long beards. The boys would all be wearing yarmulkes and prayer shawls. The women and girls would be dressed alike, with their heads covered in preparation for prayer.

My children and I would have the same conversation each time we would see them. Even though we knew we would encounter them, it was always a bit shocking to see such a unique people keeping their distinctive way of life alive in the middle of a city that is world famous for its secularism and opulence.

I will confess to having a bit of Orthodox Jewish envy. One of the things I love about being part of the evangelical segment of the Christian church is that evangelicals don't mind using aspects of the culture as tools for the gospel. We don't mind placing the gospel in terms, in fashions, in images, in sounds, and even in tastes that the world understands. We are good at fitting in. But that can be its own problem: we are good at fitting in.

The church must keep considering and discerning all of the ways we are called to embody alternatives the world does not understand in its own terms. Perhaps our uniqueness will not look like black hats, side curls, and prayer shawls, but our uniqueness should look like unconditional love, a commitment to peacemaking, a bent toward forgiveness and reconciliation, a concern for justice and mercy, a hunger after the things of God, and lives that seek first the kingdom. The world needs a holy people who have learned the habits that are a foretaste of the coming kingdom.

Dirty Hands

One of my favorite moments each week is at the end of the service on Sunday when, as pastor, I am given the opportunity to pray a prayer of benediction and blessing upon the body of Christ and send the people into the world as instruments of his blessing. A friend has helped me to think of the gathering for worship and the sending into the world as the inhaling and exhaling of God. When the unique people of God are called to worship, it is as though the Almighty breathes in and draws his people close to his heart. There we are loved. There we are heard. There we are spoken to. But then

God exhales and by the breath of his Spirit sends his people into the world as salt and light.

I have been thankful for a generation or two of young people who have come along in the evangelical church and have emphasized God's call to do justice, to love mercy, and to walk in the world with humility. The church in recent centuries could become very pietistic and live out an isolated spirituality without fulfilling the call to be a blessing to both neighbors and enemies.

I have had a concern that for some churches living justly and compassionately toward hurting people has become a new strategy for church growth. I recently heard one minister say, "We are discovering that not only does love win . . . love works!" This pastor meant it works as a way to grow the church.

That may indeed be the case. Hopefully the unique love at work in the body of Christ is attractive to those who have not experienced the unconditional love and mercy of their Creator. However, we don't go into the world and get our hands dirty in acts of mercy, compassion, and justice because it "works." The church gets its hands dirty in the needs of the world because that is the kind of royal priesthood we are becoming. We are a people who love because we have been loved.

The call of the church is not to make the world a better place to live. The call is to become a community faithfully witnessing to and extending by faith the kind of life made possible only through the death and resurrection of God's Son.

Him Again

The question raised by a sense of dislocation and loss is one of God's abandonment. Is God done with us? Has God left us? Has

God forsaken us? I hope that what has *not* happened in exploring anew the biblical theme of exile is the furthering of an unnecessary pity party or the fueling of a spiritual retrenchment on the part of the church. My hope is that in embracing exile the church might discover again the beauty of being able to live and thrive as God's unique people in the world.

Years ago an important mentor in my life introduced me to a little book that has been out of print for several decades. My favorite part of Cornelis van Peursen's little book is the title: *Him Again!* In his short treatise Van Peursen wrestles with the unfamiliarity of God and his activity by the people of Israel. They had to wonder, what is this God like? In what ways is Yahweh like and unlike the other gods? How do we know when God has shown up and acted? How can we recognize the work of the Lord? In essence, Van Peursen argues that the people had to operate like master detectives sorting out the various clues they would see, and then the wise ones among them could point and say, "Look! It's Him again! It's Yahweh at work."[4]

This idea has often made me think of some of the great detectives of literary history. I love Sherlock Holmes, but when I read Van Peursen's book, I couldn't help but think about Angela Lansbury's character in the television show *Murder, She Wrote*. Each week the plot of the show is essentially the same. Jessica is invited to attend a party. By the way, if she ever shows up at your house, leave immediately because she is clearly the angel of death. Someone at the party dies. The police show up and say something such as, "This is so strange . . . so many disconnected murders. Three nights ago there was a man killed in the billiard room with a lead pipe. Two nights ago that woman was strangled in the kitchen with a rope. Last night a couple was shot dead in the conservatory with a revolver. And now here lies this poor soul murdered with the candlestick in the library. So many disconnected events!"

But then Jessica steps forward and says something such as, "Don't you see the clues, fellas? These are not disconnected happenings; they are all related. It's him! (Usually the person is the room with them.) It's him again!"

In essence, this is what Van Peursen says that Israel has to do. They have to keep deciphering the clues of Yahweh's activity in the world.

One day in the desert an old couple has a baby. They are ninety-five and one hundred years of age—way past the time possible to procreate. And yet here is Isaac—the "Son of Laughter." It's as though the crowds look on and wonder, *How does that happen? How does a couple that has been barren for so long have a child?* The wise ones, the master detectives in the crowd, say, "It's Him again! Yahweh, the One who created the universe. It's Him again!"

Moses stands before the Red Sea facing the wrath of Pharaoh, on the one hand, and facing the waters of chaos, on the other. He raises his staff, and the waters part in two. The crowds look on and wonder, *How does that happen? How does the sea open up and allow a people to enter into new life?* The wise ones, the master detectives in the crowd, say, "It's Him again! Yahweh, the One who created the universe . . . the One who gave the baby . . . It's Him again!"

In the wilderness the people are hungry and have nothing to eat. One day they wake up and there is a strange kind of daily bread covering the floor of the desert. The crowds look on and wonder, *How does that happen? How does bread show up in the wilderness and feed a great multitude?* The wise ones, the master detectives in the crowd, say, "It's Him again! Yahweh, the One who created the universe . . . the One who gave the baby . . . the One who parted the sea . . . It's Him again!"

The story could go on this way—the walls of Jericho fall, a shepherd boy defeats a giant, a prophet calls down fire, a strange figure stands in the midst of the fiery furnace, and God meets people in the hopelessness of exile. "It's Him again! It's Him again! It's Him again!"

The story should certainly be carried forward: One day an anxious crowd stands beneath a cross upon which hangs a humble carpenter from Nazareth. The people ask, "Who is this one who came in the name of the Lord? Who is this one who made the lame dance, who made the blind see, who made the deaf hear, and who made the mute sing with joy?" The wise ones, the master detectives in the crowd, say, "It's Him again! Yahweh, the One who created the universe . . . the One who gave the baby . . . the One who parted the sea . . . the One who gave bread in the wilderness . . . the One who slayed Goliath . . . The One who rescued the Hebrew children . . . It's Him again!"

If I could conclude with one last thought, it would be this. When the world looks upon a people called the church, who are experiencing various levels of uncertainty, fears, and dislocation and yet are able to release with joy all that has happened in the past in order to receive the new thing God wants to do; when the crowds witness a people from every tribe, nation, and language embracing exile and becoming a people who uniquely reflect the grace and mercy of God to the world, the wise ones, the master detectives in the crowd, will say, "It's Him again!"

Questions for Discussion

- What does it mean to say that the church is the "light to the nations"?

- Which of the four missional images—embodied Word, open Table, clean hearts, or dirty hands—speaks most to you and why?

- What are the moments you have seen over which you can say, "It's Him again?"

- What do you think it would look like for the church where you are to embrace exile?

NOTES

Introduction

1. Stanley Hauerwas and William H. Willimon, *Resident Aliens: Life in the Christian Colony* (Nashville: Abingdon Press, 1989), 18.

2. Walter Brueggemann, *The Land: Place as Gift, Promise, and Challenge in Biblical Faith* (Minneapolis: Fortress Press, 2002), 115.

3. Ibid.

4. Lee Beach, *The Church in Exile: Living in Hope after Christendom* (Downers Grove, IL: InterVarsity Press, 2015), 59.

Chapter 1

1. Hauerwas and Willimon, *Resident Aliens*, 15.

2. Ibid., 15-16.

Chapter 3

1. "The X-Files: Quotes," Internet Movie Database, accessed October 20, 2016, http://www.imdb.com/title/tt0106179/quotes.

2. See Friedrich Nietzsche, *Thus Spoke Zarathustra,* trans. Walter Kaufmann (New York: Penguin Books, 1966), 25-78.

3. "Truth is what your contemporaries let you get away with" is a phrase often associated with Richard Rorty because of a similar statement he made in Richard Rorty, *Philosophy and the Mirror of Nature* (Princeton, NJ: Princeton University Press, 1979), 176.

4. Friedrich Nietzsche, *The Gay Science,* in *The Portable Nietzsche,* trans. Walter Kaufmann (New York: Penguin Books, 1968), 95.

5. N. T. Wright, "How Can the Bible Be Authoritative?" *Vox Evangelica* 21 (1991): 7-32.

6. Ibid.

7. Fanny Crosby, "Blessed Assurance," Hymnary.org, http://www.hymnary.org/text/blessed_assurance_jesus_is_mine.

Chapter 4

1. Tony Campolo, *Let Me Tell You a Story* (Nashville: Word, 2000), 81-82.

2. James K. A. Smith, *You Are What You Love: The Spiritual Power of Habit* (Grand Rapids: Brazos Press, 2016), 1-2.

Chapter 5

1. See Abraham Kuyper, *Lectures on Calvinism: The Stone Lectures of 1898* (Peabody, MA: Hendrickson Publishers, 2008).

2. Abraham Kuyper, "Sphere Sovereignty," in *Abraham Kuyper: A Centennial Reader*, ed. James D. Bratt (Grand Rapids: Eerdmans, 1998), 488.

3. N. T. Wright, *Surprised by Hope: Rethinking Heaven, the Resurrection, and the Mission of the Church* (New York: HarperOne, 2008), 293.

4. Ibid., 193.

Chapter 7

1. Rodney Clapp, *A Peculiar People: The Church as Culture in a Post-Christian Society* (Downers Grove, IL: InterVarsity Press, 1996), 163.

2. See Hauerwas and Willimon, *Resident Aliens*, 43-48.

3. Stanley Hauerwas, *A Community of Character* (Notre Dame, IN: Notre Dame Press, 1981), 10.

4. Cornelis van Peursen, *Him Again!* (Richmond, VA: John Knox Press, 1969).

Share the words of **hope** from *Embracing Exile* **with your** faith **community!**

ISBN: 978-0-8341-3646-5

This 7-week small group kit, including weekly videos and leader's guide, will help your community discover what faithfulness looks like and how holiness is possible, even when the surrounding culture does not affirm Christ as Lord.

Available at BeaconHillBooks.com

EMBRACING EXILE

WORSHIP MUSIC FOR YOUR JOURNEY

Songs from writers and artists, including

Jon Nicholas

Sharon Norman

Nick Robertson

Allison Durham Speer

RECORDINGS AVAILABLE ON iTUNES®

Lead sheets available for your worship team at lillenas.com